You Can't Take Them With You

Megan Bannon

To Connor & Susanna,
    With love and laughter!

Megan B

ISBN (Print): 978-0-9976380-4-2

ISBN (ebook): 978-0-9976380-3-5

Library of Congress Control Number: 2024918478

Printed in the United States of America

For Annicka, Mankow, the team at Vanderbilt who saved my life, and my husband, David, who I couldn't have gotten through this without.

Contents

Preface

Cancer is not funny. It is an asshole. It fucking sucks.

It took my grandma, my mom's mom, Arlene Means, too young.

Cancer took two of my very good friends while I was undergoing treatment. They were my cancer mentors, sadly. Talking through lab reports, treatments, side effects, and just the general hell of going through this awful, shared experience. Mankow died from melanoma after a seven-year battle, and Annicka from Stage 4 colon cancer after a nearly two-year battle that ended in her brain. Neither of them made it to forty. There is nothing fair or funny about that.

My friend Erin, another cancer mentor, had gone through breast cancer in her early thirties. She was diagnosed ten days after getting married. She was a rock for me throughout as well. Knowing exactly what I was going through. She even got the same reconstruction surgery that I am planning on as I write this book. This was after two different sets of silicone implants. One that had to be replaced because they linked them to lymphoma – perfect for a post-cancer patient. And the other because they timed out. They have to be replaced every ten years. Erin decided after dealing with both of those scenarios to have a different reconstruction that was not available when she was going through breast cancer over a decade ago. What she has taught me is that even though treatment is over and the cancer cells are gone, cancer never really leaves your life once you have it.

Another friend, Tracy, would be diagnosed with breast cancer as I was going through it all. She had her own harrowing time after her surgery. Her body refused to heal, which happens often after chemo. For weeks she had to wear a vacuum machine attached to her wounds to help her heal. The trauma from that experience made her change her mind about reconstruction. Then our friend John would be diagnosed with an extremely rare form of kidney cancer. The world-renowned doctors at the University of Chicago don't even know what to do with him. His only option is to travel to Washington, D.C., every three weeks for an experimental treatment at the National Institute of Health. Cancer everywhere, and we are all impacted directly or indirectly by it.

I am lucky. To say I am insanely grateful that I am still alive is an understatement. Cancer is unpredictable and regardless of the outcome, it takes a huge toll on patients and those who love them. Now I find myself as the cancer mentor.

The fear, pain, and stress of cancer is real and not something to be taken lightly. At thirty-eight, with a husband, two young kids (five and eight), a thriving career in advertising, and a lot of life ahead of me, I received a diagnosis of one of the most aggressive forms of breast cancer (triple-negative). Triple-negative, as I came to learn, is very hard to treat. It can often be chemo-resistant, and there are no targeted treatments for it. Googling at the time of my diagnosis told me there was over a three-in-ten chance I would be dead within five years. Luckily, these stats were out of date and there are better options that had been approved, even within the last twelve months before I was diagnosed. Regardless, this sent shockwaves through my life. There was a very real chance that I would die from this, leaving my family and friends, and missing all the things we hoped for our children.

As I settled into my diagnosis and started treatment, the paralysis lessened, and I found myself looking for the light in this dark experience. I found it through a hell of a lot of support from my family, friends, and colleagues, as well as through a lens of humor. This book reflects how laughter helped me cope with sixteen rounds of chemo, eleven rounds of immunotherapy, a double mastectomy, and thirty rounds of radiation. Not to mention the major reconstruction surgery and other subsequent surgeries that I haven't even had yet that I will need to make my body whole as it can be again.

Please don't let the humor take away from the seriousness of cancer. It upends and takes people's lives. The stories here are excerpts of a much larger year-long emotional roller coaster that was filled with scary, sad, and painful moments for me, my family, and my friends. As I write this, while my active treatment has ended, the journey has not. I still have multiple surgeries ahead of me. Every six months or so I will be scanned to look for cancer that could pop up anywhere in my body if, somehow, we didn't get it all during treatment. I won't be considered cured until I'm cancer-free for five years. Only then will my chances of long-term survival be

98%. What they don't tell you is that cancer is never really over. While the malignancies might be gone from my physical body for now, cancer is not something that ever really leaves you. There are also the long-term side effects of the treatments themselves. The chronic fatigue that can persist for years. The external scarring from my chemo port and mastectomy. The internal scarring of my left lung from radiation. The emotional toll of processing the betrayal of my own body and an attempt to put myself back together after it all.

I welcome you to laugh with me and hope that it can bring some light and guttural laughs to what no doubt is a difficult topic. Please share this with people who might benefit from the hope that comes from finding those rays of sunshine through the clouds, even if those rays are few and far between.

And please, please, please know your body and advocate for it. Especially the under-fifty folks whose rates of cancer are skyrocketing. Professionals don't always listen when younger people tell them something is wrong. This is especially true for women and people of color. You know your body better than anyone else, so don't hesitate to push, ask, and keep seeking answers if you are being brushed off. Do the damn check-ups, the skin checks, the breast checks, the colonoscopies. They suck and are annoying, but they do save lives. If you take nothing else from this book, make those appointments now if you are behind schedule.

On the first of every month, check for lumps in your breasts and under your arms. This goes for both women and men, because it turns out that men can get breast cancer too. Not to be alarmist, but if you experience unexpected bleeding, changes in your bathroom habits, or a spot on your skin, get it checked out. Chances are it's nothing, but if it is something, the earlier that you can find and treat cancer, the better your chances of survival.

Know the classic signs of colon cancer: changes in your bowel habits, anemia, and blood in your stools. Know what a normal mole on your skin looks like, and what isn't normal. If you have a mole that is changing and gets bigger than a pencil eraser, is oddly shaped, feels like sandpaper, or turns blood red, get it checked!

When I was diagnosed, I asked my oncologist if she had been seeing a rise in younger patients, because I had two other peers with cancer at the same time. She said, "yes at an alarming rate." My cancer therapist also said that 2023 was, "the year of the under-forties." Something is going on, and no one has the answers. My oncologist said maybe it's our food, and microplastics are definitely on the suspect list. The experts don't know what is happening or why, so it's up to us to be body-aware and keep up with the screenings. Thanks for listening to my Public Service Announcement.

Introduction

Let me set the stage. I was thirty-eight years old. My husband, David, and I had just celebrated our twelfth wedding anniversary. We had two kids, Baz, who was a Pokémon & LEGO-loving third grader. Eva was my whimsical pre-k-er who believed in unicorns, mermaids, and Jesus. And our thirteen-year-old Goldendoodle, Matilda, who had been part of our family since before we were even engaged. We lived in a nice house in Nashville, Tennessee, with an organic vegetable garden and a trampoline. We were talking about getting chickens. I ate healthy and exercised just like you are supposed to do. I had a big job as the Global Director of Brand Strategy at Indeed where I was working on global advertising campaigns and getting to travel overseas occasionally. I had recently had some big professional wins and thought a promotion was on the horizon. Overall, I was living a nice and normal life. The only real health risk I had was very well-controlled Type 1 diabetes that I had been living with since I was eight. Thanks to the amazing technology in modern insulin pumps and continuous glucose monitors, I never have had any major complications from it. Sure, like many moms, I had the occasional fantasy of a quick bout of appendicitis. I dreamt it would land me a few solo days in the hospital away from the pressures of two kids, a husband, and a boss. I pictured myself lying in bed all day reading a book, while people brought me food, and gentle meds rocked me to sleep.

Then one day I felt a lump in the upper part of my left breast. I didn't think that much of it because I had just been to the gynecologist a few months before and she had given me a thorough breast exam. I let it fester. It didn't seem to be getting any bigger but there was this little bug in the back of my mind that told me it was something. I continued to brush it off for a little while longer, because cancer doesn't happen to thirty-eight-year-olds living their best life.

Then the unthinkable happened.

After a multi-week diagnosis ordeal that I'll explain later in greater detail, a notification popped up in MyChart, my online medical records portal, on my phone saying that a test result was in. Being the impatient person that I was, I had been waiting for this for days, so I immediately opened it. I had been warned that the doctor would receive the lab report at the same time as I did, so they tried to help me be prepared if I chose to open it. There were a lot of words in the lab report that I didn't understand, but the one word I did know was "malignant." It was breast cancer. My immediate Googling told me that this wasn't the good kind of breast cancer (as if there is a good kind of cancer). It was the worst kind of breast cancer: triple-negative breast cancer, or TNBC. When a doctor did call me later that day, I would learn that they were so alarmed by my diagnosis ("she's thirty-eight and it's TNBC!"), that they would get me in to see the best medical oncologist on staff the next day. Dr. Abramson came in early the next morning specifically to see me before her regular appointments. Things rarely move this fast in the medical world, cancer included.

TNBC accounts for about 10-15% of all breast cancers and is the most aggressive and least treatable. In medical lingo, I was ER-negative, PR-negative and

HER2-negative. Which meant that no hormones or specific proteins were feeding my cancer, ruling out targeted treatment options. It also meant a worse prognosis. My luck.

Faced with the reality of death for the first time in my life, I imagined my kids growing up under the sole influence of my husband. They would only know how to tell dad jokes, leave their dirty socks by couch to annoy their future partners, and learn his disdain for vegetables. I imagined how much my friends and family would miss me. Who else was going to initiate drunken naked dips in large bodies of water if I wasn't there with my best friends from college? So I did what any person would do and turned to prescription anxiety drugs and non-prescription pot gummies. But that didn't quite make up for the fact that my life was completely on hold and maybe even over. That's when compartmentalization and dark humor became my savior.

As my medical plan to combat cancer became clearer, I realized that the next six months of my life were on hold, and I started to come to grips with what was happening. I would be doing weekly chemo for twelve sessions and then four more sessions of chemo every three weeks. The anxiety drugs and pot were kicking in.

I started therapy with a psychologist who specializes in cancer patients. The humor started poking through the tears and shock. At this point all the people who mattered to me knew what was happening. I was settling into my new reality, so I started to ask myself, how do you simultaneously be a sick cancer patient while having a little fun along the way? That's when my instincts as a career strategist and constant jokester kicked in, and I came up with a plan.

Strategy #1: To the best of my ability, pretend like nothing was wrong. My therapist said that this was a healthy way to cope. Just put one step in front of the other, ignore what's happening, get through treatment, then deal with the trauma after the fact. No doubt this is something I'll be dealing with in therapy for years to come. Unpacking those repressed feelings, and processing everything that happened over my nine months of treatment, and the permanent scars and side effects won't come cheaply. Way to play the long game, therapists of America!

Strategy #2: Find the light. This didn't mean finding God or beauty in the situation. Cancer is fucking ugly. And it certainly didn't mean "go to the light." No, I would use my sarcastic, occasionally macabre, sense of humor to keep smiling. It meant laughing when it was appropriate and, often, when it was not.

Luckily for me, I had a partner in crime for the journey. My husband has a similar sense of humor and could make me laugh through the worst of it. Like the time when we were having a very serious conversation about my posthumous wishes should the worst actually happen, and he threatened to give me a KISS-themed (yes like the band) funeral. More about that later.

So while I become cured meat, I captured a comedic memoir of my journey. Recalling the humorous moments, giving bites of insight into my chemo fuzzy brain, and adding humor to the things that perplexed me (like how did adult coloring books make their way on the must-have gift list for cancer patients?)

98.7% of this is 100% true.

Laughter worked for me as I slogged through nine months of grueling treatment. I emerged at the end N.E.D. (No Evidence of Disease). One of the lucky ones whose tumor responded to treatment completely. While this means great things for my prognosis, my journey is not over. I must be cancer-free for five years before I'm considered "cured," or another four years at the time of writing this book.

Talk about a cliffhanger.

Chapter One

The Time WebMD™ Was Right

We've all been there. You've been feeling fatigued for a few weeks, and there's a bruise that seems to have come out of nowhere. You type said symptoms in the WebMD™ Symptom Tracker. It generates a list of possible ailments. It could be stress, an infection, or cancer. Whatever it is, you are dying.

In my case, I had discovered a lump. Exactly when I first felt it, I can't pinpoint. But I knew it hadn't been there a few months before when I went to my gynecologist for my annual check-up. It wasn't the first time I'd had a lump in one of my breasts. The time before, I went through the motions. I had a biopsy, and all came back normal. That time I had been alarmist, as I was breast-feeding my first baby, so this time I tried not to be. Just another benign lump. No need to make an emergency out of it. I would have it checked at some point.

A few weeks later, it happened to be October, which is also Breast Cancer Awareness Month. I was scrolling through my Apple newsfeed when I came across a *People Magazine* article about a woman who found her own lump. She thought it was nothing but went to the doctor, just in case. It turned out she had cancer. Her action saved her life. I'm embarrassed to say this, but a *People Magazine* article saved mine (I'm more of a *Vanity Fair* girl.) Because of that article, I called for a doctor's appointment and got in the next day.

My regular doctor was on vacation, so I was seen by a resident (read: "junior doctor") and her supervisor (read: "I will not let her kill you"). They both agreed that my lump didn't seem too suspicious, as "it wasn't *that* hard and seemed to be moveable," but out of an abundance of caution, and to avoid any future lawsuits, I'm sure, they would send me for imaging the next day. At this point, I hadn't even told my husband anything was going on. I'm the family hypochondriac. I didn't want to take shit when, like always, this was nothing.

The next day, I had a mammogram. While the techs are very nice and try hard to put you at ease, it wasn't a very comforting experience. They smashed my boobs one by one in between cold plates while I stood in awkward poses with my arms in different positions. Sometimes having to repeat the process if the image wasn't clear enough on first take. And just when I thought I was done with that part of the ordeal, I got called back for more images. Then, they ordered an ultrasound. An ultrasound is an equally awkward situation where you lay face up on an exam table with your boobs out, but much more physically comfortable than a mammogram. No boob smashing, just some warm gel and a wand going around in circles on your boob. Borderline nice if you are into that type of thing. That is until the tech called the radiologist in. The look on the radiologist's face told me everything I needed to know. Radiologists aren't known for their interpersonal skills, but she dryly explained that she was taking a look at what they saw on the images. Immediately her gaze became stern, concerned and all eye contact was lost. It was clear, I was dying. But, then again, *statistically,* worrisome imagery is more likely *not* to be cancer than it is to be cancer. Maybe the radiologist comes in for every ultrasound? (They don't.) Not only did they find something abnormal in my left breast where the lump was, they also found something on the other breast. A splattering of calcifications that could be indicative of cancer as well.

Let me tell you, anytime that they take you into an office behind closed doors instead of the regular office check-out window, it is not a good thing. After I got dressed, that's exactly what happened. They took me into an office, closed the door, and told me they needed to schedule two biopsies, one on each side. "It's the only way we can be absolutely sure if it is cancer or not." Even worse, at this point it was early November and we were running up against the Thanksgiving holiday. It would be eighteen days before they could get me in to do both biopsies. I walked out of the breast center panicked and overwhelmed. Sobbing as I walked to the car, I called David and told him what was going on. He reassured me that no matter what happened he loved me and would be there for me. Then he asked if I was okay to drive. I took a few minutes to clear my eyes and wipe the snot from my face before I got on the road. Then I went to pick up the kids.

This is the absolute worst-case scenario for a hypochondriac who is also a skilled researcher. Over those next eighteen days, I would read everything the internet had to say about breast cancer. Me and the MyChart app would become best friends as I would read the radiologist's report enough times that I could recite it at an open mic.

You bet your ass I Googled everything. Exactly what they tell you not to do. What were the chances it was actually cancer? How quickly would I die if it were cancer? Ask me anything you'd like to know about how they grade tumor imaging for potential cancer risk. I can tell you. But I didn't stop researching there. I started playing with statistical calculators online. They graded both of my suspicious images RAD 4 (the RAD scale is how they rate the suspiciousness of a particular image for cancer. It goes from 1-5, with 1 being not suspicious at all and 5 being confirmed malignancy). I input RAD 4 into one calculator, and it showed that there was between a 10% and 80% chance that I had cancer. Given that it was in both of my breasts, I split the difference and figured it was more like a 40% chance I had cancer in one or both of my breasts. I wasn't loving the numbers, but they were optimistic for a hypochondriac. Again, statistics were, in theory, on my side.

Still, I couldn't stop! What *kind* of breast cancer could it be? Before all of this, I didn't even realize there were different types of breast cancer, but I learned that there are breast cancers fueled by hormones, and others fueled by specific proteins. Then there are subtypes depending on where it originated. Breast cancer that originates in the milk ducts is ductal or there's lobular breast cancer that originates in a mammary gland. Not to mention the various stages the cancer could be, depending on whether it had spread already or not. Then based on all of that, what treatments are available? And, of course, what was the prognosis? In those eighteen days, I became a doctor capable of giving that resident a run for her money. I also became a pharmacist because self-medicating was how I semi-managed to hold it together.

I say "semi-managed" because I had some meltdowns during this period. One is seared into my memory. My husband and I were attending a school fundraiser. The fundraiser took place at the local planetarium and included an open bar and a concert under the stars. It was going to be a lovely evening and an enjoyable event. We were ready early so pre-gamed the fundraiser at a nearby bar, as you do when you have a kid-free night out. I had one dirty martini, which turned into some very dirty tears. David helped me collect myself and calm down enough to go to the concert, but I can't imagine that people didn't notice my tear-streaked face and how absent I appeared. At this point, David was the only person who knew what I was going through and that I had two biopsies coming up.

When biopsy day finally arrived, I decided—like an idiot—that I was fine to go by myself. Being Type 1 diabetic, I'm used to handling medical appointments on my own. Plus, this wasn't my first needle biopsy, so I didn't think it would be bad. I was wrong. I actually was having two types of biopsies that day. The first one is what they call a stereotactic biopsy, during which they administer a mammogram in the biopsy room to determine the exact spot where the biopsy is needed. Lying on my stomach, I had my boob smashed between plates while they took the images. Then I dare not move a millimeter for 45 minutes as they poked and plodded, occasionally taking a sample to the next room to inspect under a microscope to make sure they got exactly what they were looking for.

That was boob one. Next up: the needle biopsy on the other side. This wasn't a nice gentle needle biopsy like the one I had before (they were in and out before I could notice). No, this doctor was moving the needle, and by "needle" I mean a quarter-inch steel rod that's hollowed out in the middle, in and out, poking holes in my lump like it was a Subway loyalty punch card. When I sat up from that one, my heart was racing, and I was shaking, apparently because the lidocaine that they had injected into my breast to numb it before the needle was inserted had adrenaline in it. They bandaged me up, and gave me two ice packs for my bra. Then I was sent home with instructions not to shower or do any exercise for 24 hours, and to change my bandages for the next few days as needed.

Then came the real wait. My Biopsy Day was two days before Thanksgiving. This was special for two reasons. First, my parents were coming in that afternoon from Dallas. We only see them every few months. Second, all the doctors and hospital staff would be taking off for the holidays, which would likely delay my results. And you already know how good I am at patiently waiting and not doom scrolling.

I fully employed Strategy #1: pretend everything is okay and deal with the fallout later. When my parents arrived that afternoon, I pretended like everything was normal. I made sure to stay on top of the gauze in my bra that ensured I wasn't bleeding out of my boobs all over my shirt like I was in a horror movie. I kept up with my pain meds, so I wasn't grimacing every time I moved. I didn't tell my parents that anything was going on. I didn't want them to worry, until I knew there was something to worry about. Especially my mom, whose mother died of breast cancer.

It was a Thanksgiving like any other, with a bustling kitchen and family gathered around the table, except I was self-medicating with wine to manage the stress, and obsessively checking MyChart every few minutes to see if the results had been published. Six days later, I saw the results before a doctor had a chance to call. And wouldn't you know it, the first doctor to call me was that fill-in resident junior doctor who said it wasn't anything to worry about. "Don't worry, it's really small," she said.

Turns out, it wasn't "really small." It was actually quite large as far as breast tumors go, coming in at 4 cm, or about 1.5 inches. Plus, it was the worst kind of breast cancer there is: triple-negative. But "good news, the other, *hold still while we smash your boobs and cut them*, side was clear." Yeah, good news.

The way the resident and her supervisor handled the situation was poor from the beginning. While I understand that gynecology isn't oncology, I'm fairly certain that most doctors have some understanding of what cancer is and what a diagnosis could mean. From the starting gate, "It doesn't feel like cancer," through to "don't worry, it's really small," there was no consideration in how I was treated. WebMD™ actually did a better job. Those doctors really should be worried that AI will take their jobs.

She didn't even tell me what my results meant or what the next steps were. Maybe they just didn't believe that a thirty-eight-year-old could have breast cancer. Maybe I'm asking too much by expecting her to understand the difference between a lab test sample size and the actual tumor size. Even the fact that the resident was the one to call and deliver the news and not my regular doctor, or even the attending, still baffles me.

Anyway, that was the day I won the statistical lottery and vindicated Web MD™. It turned out it *was* cancer, and I *was* dying.

Chapter Two

Delivering the News with Grace

Typically the next thing that happens after you receive a cancer diagnosis is you have to start telling people. You certainly can't go too long without people noticing that your hair has fallen out, amongst other telltale signs. The process is quite the effort that typically starts with your closest family and friends and then goes from there.

In my case, my parents happened to still be in town when I received my diagnosis since it was right after Thanksgiving. We thought it would be in pretty bad taste to wait for them to get home and then tell them over the phone given that we knew and they were there. Knowing that they were going to lose their shit, we wanted to meet with the oncologist before we gave them the news. We wanted to understand what we were dealing with and go in with a plan, so we could be as prepared as possible for this conversation.

On the morning of their departure, I told them that I had found a new endocrinologist and they had an opening in their schedule. I got in my car and went straight to the Vanderbilt Breast Center. David got in his car and took the kids to school drop-off. He would meet me at the breast center as quickly as he could. Alone at first, the oncologist, Dr. Abramson, brought me back almost immediately. I told her David would be here shortly, and then immediately burst into tears. She reassured me that things were going to be okay. The first thing she told me was that the statistics on prognosis that you can find on Google are dated. Even in the past year, significant leaps in treatment had been made. She wasn't going to let me die. David arrived shortly thereafter, and Dr. Abramson got out a pad of paper and a pen and wrote out the plan. Twenty-four weeks of chemo. Twelve of them weekly with two drugs. And the last four every three weeks with a different set of drugs. And every three weeks through-out this period (and we would later learn beyond) the immunotherapy drug, Keytruda™. After that surgery (in my case, a double mastectomy.) Then six weeks of radiation. The next nine months of my life all planned out.

All of this would begin less than two weeks later on December 15. We were then ushered off to meet with the cancer pharmacist who would give us a bunch of reading materials on the specific drugs I would be taking. Armed with a plan and our bedtime reading, we got in our cars and drove home. We both pulled into the garage, took a deep breath, and walked into the house together.

We made it home just as my parents were rolling out their suitcases. The perfect time to tell them I had cancer. Give them the news, chuck them into the car, and send them on their merry way. Execution of this well-thought-out plan went something like this:

"Mom, Dad, we need you to sit down."

"No really, please sit down."

Parents reluctantly comply.

I blurt out, "I have breast cancer."

Complete shock ensues. Their faces go white and all expression goes blank. My dad starts crying. An awkward pause happens, and then we embrace each other in a big hug. At the time I thought they probably thought I was pregnant with a third child. No, I learned later, they thought we were getting a divorce.

With panicked energy, "Don't worry! I am going to be okay. It's only stage 2. We have a plan. I start chemo in fifteen days! Alright, we gotta leave for the airport. Please get in the car."

With David driving, we take the longest, most awkward fifteen-minute drive of my life. Silence.

I know my parents are panicking but are trying to hold it together for me. I secretly cannot wait for this to be over. Finally, we pull up to curbside check in.

The usual hugs and goodbyes happen. I get back in the car, and as we are driving away, I yelled out the passenger side window, "Get a Bloody Mary on the plane, Mom, you're gonna need it!"

• • •

For anyone who finds themselves in this situation, when it's time to deliver the news to your kids, here's what I recommend doing. Ignore the fact that they are five and eight years old respectively and take them to a fancy sushi restaurant. Sit them down, and as the waiter is filling your water glasses, have your husband or partner blurt out, "Mommy has cancer!"

Mommy will immediately begin sobbing. The eight-year-old will too. The five-year-old will ask, "Can I watch a movie on your phone?", and the waiter will stand there in shock, nearly overfilling the water glasses. Not knowing what to make of this very awkward situation we have just put him in, he will just sort of look at you with his mouth agape until you turn to him with your drink order.

As the dinner goes on, you will try to explain to your children (and really just the older one because the five-year-old is lost in the land of Disney+) that you *probably* won't die. You'll explain that the doctors are super smart. The treatments have come a long way. Yes, life is going to be a bit different for a while and Mommy is going to look and act a bit different for a while. It's all temporary while she gets better. But don't worry about that, go ahead and order that extra $20 sushi roll you really want to, and get a Shirley Temple while you are at it. We are living it up tonight!

Meanwhile, the waiter will keep dropping off extra dishes from the kitchen, while awkwardly explaining that they overheard the news and thought that some unagi with truffle-soy glaze would make everyone feel better!

Your husband will comment that "you should get cancer all the time," because he's jazzed about all the free stuff that suddenly is coming our way.

The dinner will end with simultaneous tears of terror and amusement, while snot runs down your face.

Unsure if the snot was caused by wasabi or cancer, you'll think to yourself, "one day we will laugh about this."

• • •

Then came telling my friends. This was messy and involved a lot of crying. First there was my best friend, Kim. She's the sister I never had. We were random college roommates freshman year and have been inseparable ever since. She was the maid of honor in my wedding. I stood up in hers. She's my ride or die, the first person I call with all the highs and lows that life has to give. We had always joked that I would die in some freak tragic accident such as getting hit by a Krispy Kreme donut truck. It would be perfect and ironic, as it wouldn't be my love for donuts that finally clogged my arteries and killed me, it would be the vehicle that delivers them. It was never supposed to be cancer.

For some reason that I can't remember, I recall pacing around our guest bedroom when I had a lot of these conversations. Each one started with a text:

Urgent. Can you talk?

When each friend called, I broke the news, and we talked about the plan. More specifics are lost on me honestly because that was such a hazy time.

Then there were my friends who currently had cancer and some that were survivors. That was more akin to joining a secret society. I had the password to join the underground club. These conversations were extra hard because I knew that they didn't wish this upon anyone, but of course they all jumped into action and instantly became my cancer guides on this terrible journey. Annicka, Erin, and Mankow were the people I could be the most real with because they knew exactly what I was going through. I am forever grateful for benefiting from their knowledge and wisdom. They knew exactly how I was feeling and told me exactly what to ask and do. They had amazing advice such as to suck on Gatorade ice cubes during chemo to keep the mouth sores away.

As news does, it started making its way to my extended family and friend groups. Text messages, calls, emails, and even snail mail started making their way to me. The love poured in. It was a humbling response that I didn't think I deserved. Some people choose to keep their cancer secret. My oncologist told me that even just a few years ago she would see patients in the real world, and they would ignore her because they didn't want people to know that they had cancer. But that culture was changing, and I was there for it. I needed people to know what was going on because I knew that I wasn't going to be myself or be able to show up how I did before. Mostly I needed a rock-hard foundation to be under me while I fought the hardest battle of my life. Unfortunately, since most of this was done via electronic communication, there was no free sushi for telling my friends I had cancer.

Chapter Three

Cancer Hell Week

When you get inducted into the secret cancer society, there is a hazing week I have deemed Cancer Hell Week. This is an absolute blur of a week filled with a flurry of appointments, tests, and even a minor surgery.

I was diagnosed on a Monday. On Tuesday I met with my medical oncologist, and we made the plan. On Wednesday, I had blood drawn for genetic testing to see if I had any genetic markers that would predispose me to breast or other cancers and then influence the treatment plan (I didn't). That day, I also had a CT scan to look at the rest of my organs and see if cancer was anywhere else. I also got to meet the breast surgeon, who would eventually perform my double mastectomy.

You Can't Take Them with You

Good news, she was available to install my chemo port tomorrow, Thursday!

The chemo port makes delivering chemo easier and ensures that you don't kill your veins in the process of all the blood draws required throughout chemotherapy. It's essentially a catheter that is inserted into your vena cava vein right next to your heart. It requires a minor surgery to insert. Sometimes they do this with what they call twilight anesthesia, during which you remain partially awake and aware of what is going on. When the anesthesiologist talked to me about the plan, I had an absolute freak out about the idea of being awake while they cut into my chest and neck, especially after my biopsy traumas. She promised me the champagne treatment and I was rolled away. When I woke up a bit later, the nurse in the recovery room proclaimed, "Wow the anesthesiologist must have really liked you. She gave you Fentanyl!"

But wait, there's more! On Friday I went for an MRI to have a closer look at my tumor and the surrounding lymph nodes. Then I drove across town to the main hospital to have an echocardiogram of my heart. This was to ensure my heart was healthy before receiving the "Red Devil" chemo that can cause heart damage. Of course the fun didn't just end there, turns out it looked like there was cancer in at least one of my lymph nodes. I begged my oncologist to assume that it was cancer and move on, but she said they needed to confirm if it was or wasn't, because it would change the treatment plan if it was. More bad news, I was going to need another biopsy.

This biopsy was the needle kind again. It was gentler than the first needle biopsy, and the radiologist who performed it was very calming, knowing that I already had been diagnosed with cancer. By the time I met with my oncologist again, a week after I met her, all of this was done. The lymph node did have cancer. My cancer diagnosis was upgraded to stage 2b. Not the kind of upgrade that comes with a bigger seat and a free drink.

Somehow, I made it through this hazing week and had another week or so to recover before starting chemo. The good news, the cancer wasn't visible anywhere else in my body, and I now knew the secret handshake.

Chapter Four

Winning the Lottery

Once the news was out in the world, people came out of every crevice and crack of my life, present and past. It was exactly like what you hear happens when someone wins the lottery. Except instead of being asked for money, I was being showered with love. It came from even the most unexpected places. The incredible outpouring from the get-go on my cancer journey no doubt showed me that I was valued as a friend, a co-worker, a daughter, a niece, a cousin– a human being.

First came a video. Our friends Ann and Brad, who had been our old neighbors and with whom we had traveled with many times, sent a Cameo when they heard the news. Cameos are short, personalized videos that celebrities make for people on demand. Mine was from the Island Boy, a set of extremely tattooed brothers who became popular on YouTube for their ridiculous hip-hop songs. They were a running joke within our friend group, and a staple of our beachside trips. It brought a much-needed smile during Cancer Hell Week.

There was the blanket that my daughter's preschool teachers sent home for me to comfort me during my chemo sessions. The cookies from a friend in the United Kingdom, whom we hadn't seen in years. The orchid my Aunt Sue and Uncle Randy sent that I tried desperately to keep alive, but even though it claimed it only needed a few ice cubes a week to live, and I dutifully gave this thing its ice, I still couldn't keep it alive. To be fair, the orchid could have tried a little harder.

Then there were the snail mail cards, like the one my college roommate and best friend Kim's parents sent. Or the one from my colleague's mom, whom I had only met once. My friend Tracy sent me a weekly card in the mail. The cards were always hilarious and were a constant source of spirit lifting.

A group of friends who were all connected through past jobs in Chicago, called the Countertop Club (this all started so we could see our friend Mary's new countertops while drinking wine, hence, the Countertop Club), sent me love at every step of the journey. Things to make chemo more comfortable, celebratory items when I had gotten through each stage of treatment, surgery prep, and more celebrations when I was finally declared N.E.D. A group of colleagues from my team organized to send the kids science and craft kits from Kiwi & Company so they would have inside activities to do and keep their minds off having a sick mom. Another colleague, Greta, organized a care package from the creative team at work that included the book, *I Hope This Finds You Well,* by Kate Baer. Along with a fancy-looking pill case (they do exist), and a gift certificate to Whole Foods so I could order healthy meals. The book was not only hilarious, but it is also part of what inspired me to write mine. My best girlfriends from college sent me a beautiful leather handbag at the end of my treatment to celebrate and remember the day I was cancer-free.

My friend Erin who was a breast cancer survivor and had gone through all the same motions in her mid-twenties was a constant source of support and a sounding board through it all and beyond.

My mom flew here from Dallas on multiple occasions to be with me, help with the kids, and the house. She even stayed for two weeks after my mastectomy since I was going to be down a set of hands with the lifting and movement restrictions after that surgery. One of my best friends from high school, Megan, and her family, used some precious days off to visit us in Nashville and help. Another really good friend, K.T., came when it was all over so we could celebrate together. Many others offered to come if we needed anything, and I know they meant it.

There are countless other gestures of kindness, love, and support that I received that could fill a whole book themselves if I listed them out here. I saved every single note and card that I received during those nine months of my life. Recently, as I was looking through the pile, which is over three inches deep, my daughter asked me what they were. I told her, "It's all the love that people sent me when I was sick. Remember that time Mommy didn't have any hair?"

She thought for a second, and then she asked, "Why are you saving them?"

"Good question," I responded. Then I pondered for a second, "Well I suppose I could throw them in the trash or burn them to symbolize the end of the worst period of my life. But then how would I remember not to die?"

Chapter Five

Let's Play a Game: Name Your Tumor

At this point I had been diagnosed, I had a plan, and the people who needed to know, knew. The next step to winning at cancer was naming my tumor. Just like naming a child or a dog, this is something that I knew I was going to have to live with for a while, so it needed to be carefully considered.

The naming ceremony for my tumor came after delivering the news to our kids, family, and friends. My husband and I decided to take a weekend trip to Chattanooga, which is only a few hours away from home, before I started chemo. The plan was to leave mid-afternoon on a Friday, stay at a really nice hotel, enjoy some nice meals together, and just be us one more time before everything got harder for the fore-seeable future.

Then Eva, our five-year-old, made the dumb choice to go and break her wrist on the playground that Friday. When it happened, the teachers knew what was going on, so they hesitantly called and said that she had fallen off a slide. They didn't think it was broken and she was resting after some Tylenol. Then they sent an email a bit later with some pictures, and I instantly knew that her wrist was broken. David, being David, jumped into action and immediately left to pick her up and get her to urgent care. Of course, the first place he went to didn't have an x-ray tech that day for whatever reason, so they wouldn't be able to help. He then drove about thirty minutes out of town to another urgent care where she was able to get x-rayed. Not only was her wrist broken, but it was broken in two places. Fuck. Whelp, there goes our last chance of normalcy.

Not so fast though. Grandma, who was a nurse and was going to take care of them that weekend, said she could handle it. She knew how important this weekend was for us. And so did David. So we left a few hours late and would get stuck in some Friday rush hour traffic. A little delayed, and more exhausted than planned, we made it to Chattanooga and quickly settled into our weekend away.

One night on this trip, we were lying in bed and thought it would be funny to watch the incredible 1990 classic film *Kindergarten Cop* because of Arnold Schwarzenegger's infamous line, "It's not a tumah!" It was then that we knew my tumor would be called Arnold.

The hope was that by not acknowledging that it was a tumor at all, it would be annihilated like Arnold annihilated all his enemies in his thrilling movies throughout the nineties. The Terminator said it all. It ended up being the perfect name. Like a growing baby in my belly, I would talk to my tumor. Instead of telling it how excited I was to meet it, how much I loved it, and all the dreams I had for it, I wished Arnold death on a daily basis. And as I felt my tumor shrinking (yes, I was lucky enough to feel it shrinking with chemo) I dreamt about all the things I would do once Arnold was ridden from my body.

There were many similarities between cancer and pregnancy. In both cases, to protect my compromised immune system, I wasn't allowed to eat raw or under-cooked meat or seafood. I wasn't allowed to go skiing or do anything fun that might break a bone. You should have seen the look on my oncologist's face when I asked if I could go skiing. It's an outdoor activity, it must be safe right? Wrong. I felt nauseated and exhausted every day, just like the forty long weeks of pregnancy. Even the timeline was about the same as my treatment plan was nine months long.

So that was also how I played my first cancer card and got my husband to agree that at the end of this, instead of getting a baby, I would get a puppy.

I wasn't going to walk away from cancer empty-handed.

The big question was, would we name the puppy Arnold?

Chapter Six

Blondes Have More Fun, Right?

There were about two weeks between my cancer diagnosis and starting chemo. This is a very surreal time where everything is the same, and yet nothing is normal at the same time. Everything was moving in slow motion. I was in all out denial of the situation. Moving one foot in front of the other, trying to plan for as much as I could for the unknown that was ahead of me. I found myself Googling lists of things I would need for chemo. I was also imagining what it would be like to lose my hair. Once in my freshman year of high school, I was on the swim team and all the boys were shaving their heads for a meet, because that was going to make them go milliseconds faster in the water. My coach said to me that he thought I would look good bald. I told him to shave my head and sat down in the seat to make it happen. He refused, probably fearing the wrath of my mother if he did it, so I never knew what I would actually look like bald.

With the first set of chemo, there was a pretty good chance that I would lose my hair. I would definitely lose it with the second set. So they gave me a prescription for wigs. Yes, you read that right, a prescription for a wig. They recommended I go wig shopping while I still had hair so they could match my natural look. And to be honest, I was excited about this part. I could finally go blonde or even curly. My pre-cancer hair was naturally jet black and very straight. It was a silver lining amidst the dark storm clouds that I could have some fun with no real commitment.

It was my hair, however, that my kids struggled with the most during my cancer journey. Baz, my eight-year-old math whiz, who wasn't easily rattled by things, did not think that going blonde or straying from my natural hair was a good idea. My five-year-old girlie girl worried I would have "boy" hair. She fixated on this and refused to move on (still as I'm writing this with about four inches of hair back on my head, she asks me when I will have hair again). To help them process this big change,

I promised them both that they could help me pick out a wig.

I chose a wig shop that specializes in helping cancer patients and those with alopecia (an autoimmune disorder that causes you to lose your hair). At shops like these, you make an appointment and have the whole place to yourself while you pick out the perfect wig. The whole family took the trip to the opposite side of town to make an afternoon of wig shopping together.

The process started with me showing pictures of my pre-cancer hair. At this point I had already cut it short and donated my long hair to Locks of Love, a not-for-profit organization that makes real hair wigs for children with cancer. Then we began trying things on. Short. Long. Curly. Straight. Blonde. Red. Even rainbow! I didn't love any of them. Most felt a little too, *I live in the South and go to church every Sunday,* for this non-church-goer who identifies as a Midwesterner. The shop owner kept reminding me that everything would fit better once I had no hair (*can't wait*), so I shouldn't get caught up on them feeling a bit too full. *As if that was the only thing I was stuck on.*

Perhaps I should have just said I wasn't ready to make this decision and checked out a few other places. But then, we arrived at a wig that seemed close. It was a mid-length, straight brown wig with some nice highlights. I liked that the highlights would be a new addition to my look. When my eight-year-old said that it was the one, I had to agree. It was worth the $500 price tag if it would make my kids feel better about the situation. Turns out that even though I had a prescription, insurance would only cover a fraction of the cost because this wig shop was out of network. But it was settled, this was the one we were taking home. I never did figure out a wig shop that was in-network.

I hung the wig in my closet upside down, just like the shop owner suggested and waited for my hair to fall out. Like clockwork, about two weeks into my weekly chemo sessions, my hair started falling out in clumps. In the shower I would shampoo and, like a scene from a horror movie, my hands would return from massaging my scalp full of hair.

Chapter Seven

Who Wears It Best?

It was time to shave my head and save myself from the itching and shedding that happens when you lose your hair quickly. To bring the kids along for the ride, and normalize what was happening as much as possible, we decided to make it a family head shaving affair and took a time lapse video recording of the event.

First, David shaved his head. Then he offered the same barbershop services to both children, but neither of them would take him up on it. Then it was my turn. David did most of the head shaving, but we let the kids take a turn buzzing my hair, with extreme supervision, of course. Now I was ready to debut my wig to its full potential on my now hairless head.

In my mind, I was going to wear my wig to work, and maybe out in the world anytime I didn't want to look like I have cancer—which would be most of the time. It was going to be a staple of my look. At this point in my cancer journey, I was still in a bit of denial. I'd only been through a couple of rounds of chemo. I didn't feel terrible, and even while my hair was falling out, I was trying to go about my business as usual.

So, when I put on the wig for the first time with a bald head, I thought that my hair would look even better than it did in the shop because it would sit more naturally on my head. In fact, I fully expected to love wearing wigs because I've never been one for spending much time on my hair, or anything beauty related for that matter. When the lady at the shop talked to me about natural hair wigs and told me that many women prefer them because they can still go through their regular hair routine with them, I laughed at her. The most I had ever done with my hair is wake up, shower, and comb it straight. Maybe a hair dryer or curling iron for a very special occasion. The thought that I could wake up in the morning and just throw on my hair, and it would look styled and perfect was compelling.

Once I got it on and looked in the mirror, I couldn't put my finger on it, but something wasn't right. The wig didn't feel like *me*. Then I started getting flashbacks to the time we lived in Brooklyn. The families that we would see around the neighborhood, at the Coney Island Aquarium, or on the subway. Then it dawned on me. Oh my God, I have chosen the same wig that every Hasidic Jewish woman wears. Absolutely zero offense to all my Jewish friends, but that is not the look I was going for. It was not "a hot mom denying she had cancer" look. It was a super conservative buttoned up look that shouted, "I have cancer." There was no recovering from this. Then and there I made the bold decision to just embrace the bald. I won't even bother trying to find a more suitable wig. I just stuck to the headbands, bows, and scarfs that dressed up my head a bit. You wouldn't catch me dead wearing one of those cancer hats or head coverings. Again, Strategy #1, pretend you don't have cancer and reject anything that would tell people you did. They still knew.

In the end, I wore the wig out only once in public. It was to my friend Jackie's fortieth birthday party—a fancy affair where there would be a number of people I hadn't met. I didn't want my cancer to take away from her day. To be honest, with a cute headband and some styling, it wasn't too bad, but I never wore it again.

We did, however, find a great way to put the wig to use: Who Wears It Best? It's an amazing party game, that we still break out occasionally when we have a fun-loving group of friends over.

A few pictures for your consideration:

Our friend Brian   Baby Paloma   Our dog, Mattie

Lesson learned. If I had to do it all over again, I would not go buy an expensive wig. I wish I had ignored the advice and just waited until my hair fell out to see what I was most comfortable with. For me, cancer was a temporary part of my identity. I didn't need to hide it under a wig. That was my choice, but there was no way to know that until I was there.

Chapter Eight

"Hey Siri, What Should I Send to My Friend with Cancer?"

It's the spring of 2015. The height of the adult coloring book craze is passing. A group of one of these coloring book company's executives are sitting around a board table, brainstorming how they can keep sales strong in this operating environment.

"Ok, we've penetrated the bored artsy types. Most people only need one coloring book that they'll do for a few days and then forget on their shelves. Our sales are down 78%. We have warehouses full of books that we need to get rid of. Who can we sell them to?"

"The elderly?"

"Nah, their eyesight and motor function aren't great for the small details."

"Dads? I mean, they need to relax too, right?"

"They don't have the attention span for that! It's not like they can take a coloring book and pencils into the bathroom for 20 minutes like they can their phone."

"True."

"So…"

And then, in a spark of inspiration, Mary from Marketing shouts, "Cancer patients!"

"It's brilliant! They have so much time on their hands, need an escape from reality, perhaps a little inspiration or humor to cheer them up and take their minds off cancer. Plus, it's a growing market. This is going to be BIG."

Bob from Finance chimes in, "You are so right! The total addressable market has to be huge. And with rates of cancer skyrocketing in the under-fifties, the future growth potential is HUMONGOUS!"

"And it doesn't even matter if they die because new patients are diagnosed daily. If we can convince people to send their cancer patient friends coloring books, I'd estimate each patient would receive on average 2.5 books. The numbers are IMPRESSIVE."

Bob continues to type on his calculator, then he looks up with the biggest smile we've ever seen from a finance guy EVER. "The potential annual revenue on cancer patients alone is $1 billion. And that's if I'm being conservative."

"Mary from Marketing, you are a true genius. How do we make this happen?"

· · ·

Enter 2022 and you find yourself with a friend with cancer. You want to send them something thoughtful that they really need, but you've never had cancer yourself, so you aren't really sure what to send. Luckily, you have this handy dandy thing called the internet, so you turn to your reliable pal and say, "Hey Siri, what can I send my friend with cancer?"

Siri instantly generates a series of listicles from around the internet with ideas of things people going through cancer might find useful. Meals? Obvious. Socks and hats to keep them warm? Boring. Books? Maybe. The lists will vary, but they all have one thing in common: Adult coloring books.

Bring in the copywriter: *"If your friend is going through chemo, she might be spending a lot of time in the infusion center and will need things to keep her busy and her mind off treatment. A coloring book is a great way for her to escape, tap into her inner child, and manifest positive thoughts."*

It's perfect! And even better, Siri can link you right to an Amazon page for the *Color Me Cancer Free: Nearly 100 Coloring Templates to Boost Courage and Morale During Cancer Treatment* coloring book. It doesn't get any more thoughtful than this! Add on a set of overpriced colored pencils, and your friend can waste away their days while their body gets pumped full of toxic chemicals.

• • •

Enter me, late 2022. I've been diagnosed with cancer and am about to start twenty-four weeks of chemo. To my surprise and delight, love pours in from everywhere. Letters, notes of encouragement, text messages, and gifts. So many generous gifts.

I'm trying to figure out what chemo is going to be like and Googling what to pack in a chemo bag. Snacks, cozy socks, a phone charger, a book, even an adult coloring book to help me pass the time and relax.

Then a package shows up from Amazon, and wouldn't you know it, there it is right on cue: an adult coloring book and some beautiful colored pencils. It's like someone knew. Then I get another care package, and wouldn't you know it, in it there's another coloring book. Then another. Then another. At this point I'm up to, I don't know, four or five coloring books. And three sets of pencils. But no worries. They are all slightly different and I've got twenty-four weeks of free time to discover my inner child through the relaxing art of coloring patterns. No doubt I can put them to good use.

C-Day arrives and it's time for my first treatment. In my bag, I have all my stuff, including one of my handy dandy coloring books and pencils. Additionally, I have a cooler bag filled with ice packs that I'll wear on my hands and feet during one of my treatments to ward off one of the side effects of that drug, permanent nerve damage.

I learn in that first session that a typical weekly chemo session goes something like this:

>**8:00 a.m.:** Arrival, check in at the infusion center and have labs drawn.

>**8:15-9:00 a.m.:** Wait for my labs to come back so I can see the doctor and have my meds approved. They'll text when I can see the doctor, so I try to get my steps in.

>**9:00 a.m.:** See the doctor for an average of three-and-a-half minutes.

9:30 a.m.: Check back in at the infusion center.

10:00 a.m.: Go back to my personal chemo room and start pre-meds, which help to prevent an allergic reaction, side effects, and anxiety.

10:30 a.m.: Once the pre-meds have kicked in, I start my first infusion, which takes about thirty minutes.

10:45 a.m.: Start icing my hands and feet. For the best effect, I have to start icing about fifteen minutes before I start the nerve-damaging drug.

11:00 a.m.: Start the nerve-damaging drug. Also start sucking on Gatorade ice cubes to ward off potential sores from forming in my mouth.

12:00 p.m.: Finish one drug and start another.

12:15 p.m.: Finally take the ice off my hands and feet, stop eating ice cubes. (Oh yeah, I had to keep the ice on after the treatment for fifteen minutes.)

12:45 p.m.: Finish my infusion and go home.

If you were tracking, it turns out that I had to ice my hands and feet for most of my infusion session, or about an hour and a half. In addition to that being pure torture, and me not being able to keep myself warm during that period, I couldn't use my hands while they were in the ice mittens. That meant twelve weekly sessions of chemo and zero coloring.

I'll give Mary from Marketing the benefit of the doubt though; I'm pretty sure she wouldn't have known that when she came up with her brilliant strategy.

Chapter Nine

How to Win at Cancer

Winning at cancer is more than just surviving. It means being the favorite cancer patient of all your doctors and nurses. As a lifelong teacher's pet, I had to be the one. Anyone who knows me knows that I do not lose well. So, the idea that I couldn't absolutely win over every doctor and nurse, while also winning at cancer was a complete non-starter.

This is no easy feat. Cancer is serious. So, it's a Very. Fine. Line.

First things first, break the ice

With my first twelve rounds of weekly chemo, I had to ice my hands and feet to avoid permanent nerve damage from the drugs. This sucked, as I've already pointed out. Having your extremities on ice for over an hour is not fun for many reasons. I couldn't color in one of the many books I'd been given, but worse, I couldn't play Candy Crush Saga for an hour and a half or so. After my pre-meds were administered, I'd start a countdown. I could get in maybe three rounds of Candy Crush before a nurse would come in and tell me it was time to start icing.

One day, I had a particularly fun nurse (you just know) and when she came in, I sang a little refrain of Vanilla Ice's famous rap song (for those of you not as cool as me and my nurse), "Ice, Ice, Baby" and she started cracking up saying, "I was thinking that, but I couldn't say it. But now that you've said it…". The two of us belted it out to the applause of nearby patients.

My status as her favorite was forever solidified.

Make inappropriate jokes

There is nothing sexier than being in a chemo infusion room with your partner, let me tell you. That's why when the nurses ask if you want them to dim the lights, you say, "Yes, we'd love for you to put the mood lighting on for us."

If they ask how you're feeling, reply, "living the dream." Because clearly, this was a dream and not reality.

Alternatively, you can always reply, "I'm having a really bad hair day." Which if they are a serious nurse, and not one of your favorites, will go down like a ton of bricks since you have no hair.

Most of the nurses appreciated our silly sense of humor, even though we were not in a silly environment in the least. However, there was this one nurse that over the course of twenty-four weeks, we could just not crack. She might give a polite smile, but for whatever reason, she was not willing to laugh along with our shenanigans. One point deducted from my win, but the game wasn't over.

Always request the champagne treatment, it will make THEM happy

Every cancer treatment center is different, but part of the whole chemo routine is your pre-meds. These are typically a cocktail of various anti-nausea medications, steroids, and other things to help ease the side effects of the chemo drugs. This often includes anti-anxiety medications to help you get through the whole experience. The drug in my cocktail was Ativan. A nice little champagne ride.

In my case, there were two different infusion centers that I would go to for treatment. The Vanderbilt Breast

Center and Infusion Center that we went to for most of those sessions happened to be in a converted shopping mall. Imagine an old school mall where each old store stall is dedicated to a medical specialty. Typically I would be in the old mall for my treatments, as that's where the doctors were, and it was closer to my house. There was nothing wrong with this center, but it was a little older and shabbier than the one I would go to on the fancy side of town, in Belle Meade. The old mall didn't have the massaging chairs with the warmers like they did in Belle Meade. And you didn't get to go to your room right away and just stay there for labs and everything. At the mall, I would do labs and then wait for the doctor to sign off on your chemo before I was called back to my private room. At the fancy location, everything was a bit fresher, from the calming white and lavender paint on the walls compared to the brown of the mall. The rooms were just a bit nicer. In fact, there was a celebrity going through treatment at the same time as I was, and of course she was being treated at the fancy center. So it's no surprise that there, they would always ask me if I wanted the Ativan. I would always answer "yes" of course. After all, everyone was a VIP at the Belle Meade infusion center.

At the other center, I always had to ask for it. If it was a good day, and I was assigned to one of my favorite nurses, it didn't really need to be said. But there were times where I would get one of the more serious nurses, and I would have to ask, feel judged, and just roll with it. And you can bet your ass I did. Every. Single. Time.

Why? Why not? I'm here getting pumped full of shit, why shouldn't I have a little Ativan party for a few hours a week? And I might as well get something out of this. In all honesty, when I was going through my first twelve weeks of treatment and having to ice my hands and feet, it really did help me relax and have a slight out of body experience while I was getting frostbite on my extremities. For the second twelve weeks, well I didn't *need* it per se. But again, why not? A happy patient makes a happy nurse.

Enroll them in supporting your misbehavior

On my actual last infusion, after I had finished chemo and at the end of the radiation, I got my favorite nurse. It also was the same day that my oncologist told me that I was officially N.E.D. This was a BIG day. Clearly celebrations were in order.

She asked how I would be celebrating, and I'm pretty sure I said "tequila." I'm not really a tequila drinker, but I knew she would get a kick out of it.

Instead of saying, "Hey, you just kicked cancer's ass, and now you are about to pump your body full of a bunch of stuff. Maybe you should lay off the booze, lady," she said the opposite.

"Well, in that case, we better up your fluids today!"

She was my favorite nurse the whole time, but this secured her legendary status. Those are the nurses who make getting through this shit easier. It didn't hurt that I had clearly become her favorite as well. Checkmate.

Chapter Ten

Rituals

Every Tuesday for twelve weeks, and then every third Tuesday for the next twelve, I had chemo and that crazy, frostbite-filled schedule.

My amazing husband took me to most of those sessions, which were at the old mall location.

Because of the wait between labs, the doctor's appointment, and the actual chemo, David and I essentially became mall walkers every Tuesday. The loop around the old mall is almost one-third of a mile. We always strived to make it at least a mile or thirty minutes of walking before my infusion, so I could close my Apple Watch exercise rings of course! All part of my plan to not lose at cancer.

· · ·

When chemo was over, without fail, when we got into the car after each session, he would immediately play the song "Toxic" by Britney Spears. If it happened to be one of the few times he didn't personally take me, my companion for the day was under strict instructions to make sure this ritual was not missed. The lyrics are quite fitting for after chemo because you are quite literally toxic. (My editor swears that Britney and/or the producer of the song will sue me if I put the lyrics in the book, so please Google them if you are not familiar.)

Don't worry about it, it's just toxic enough to kill the cancer (and your hair) but not toxic enough to kill you. Just don't let your loved ones come in contact with your bodily fluids. And make sure you flush the toilet twice for 48 hours after treatment so you don't accidentally poison someone who uses the bathroom after you. Oh and finally, not that anyone wants to have sex after chemo, but don't do that either for at least forty-eight hours or you will poison your partner.

The chorus of "Toxic" is very on the nose. While Britney is referring to a toxic relationship, my husband was keen to point out that my body was toxic after chemo.

Yes, David, I am very aware of how toxic I am. But I appreciate you letting Britney remind me every damn week!

• • •

After my chemo days I would be pretty wiped. So my husband, being the lovely human that he is, would leave me in my comatose state on the couch and dutifully pick up the kids from school. He would always take them to their favorite place for dinner, which also happens to be my least favorite place for dinner: Buffalo Wild Wings. I am not personally a fan of chicken wings with bones, so when forced to go there I would order the boneless ones or maybe a burger. Again, nothing redeeming about Buffalo Wild Wings for me personally, no offense to those who like it, and certainly the last thing I would want to eat after chemotherapy. It was the perfect place to go without me because the kids love it.

The funny thing about this is that my kids don't even like chicken wings either. They go there for the burger and the mac and cheese respectively. Maybe it was the mandarin oranges that come with the meal or the chocolate milk we occasionally would allow?

Regardless, my chemo days became their favorite day of the week because they got to go to B-Dubs, or whatever the kids call it these days.

Chapter Eleven

Cancer Suits You

I am one of those hidden introvert types. I'm happy to stay at home. I like to socialize, but I don't need to socialize to be happy. When I meet people, I'm a bit shy at first. This fades quickly once the social anxiety lessens. Unlike David, I don't like to actively seek out new people. When I got cancer, it wasn't the lifestyle changes we would have to make to ensure that I didn't die from a common cold that made me nervous. It was the anxiety that came with strangers knowing I had cancer. I didn't want the attention, or the pity.

At first, I didn't mind the idea of staying out of the public eye for the next six months while I was going through chemo. It was also right before Christmas, so I could cozy up by the tree and enjoy time with my kids by the fire while carols played in the background and we all sipped hot cocoa. It felt like it could be worse. Then after my first chemo treatment, my white blood cells got wiped. This meant that I had no immune system and was at major risk for getting extremely sick should I come into contact with any virus or especially bacteria. Everything was now a risk. Even my children, because all kids are disease-spreading vehicles, especially my kindergartner. Instantly the drawbridge went up, and the family and I were locked inside the castle walls. Luckily, it was Christmas break, so we didn't have to worry immediately about them bringing something home from school. But this is not the Christmas we wanted, where no one was allowed at our house, and none of us could go out in public.

The isolation was like nothing I had experienced before. Not even the darkest days of the COVID-19 pandemic compared. Turns out this introvert does need interaction and stimulation beyond the four walls and four people (I'm counting the dog) of my house. It just made something that was already extremely difficult, even more difficult because it banished my support system into the virtual cloud. In some ways, the pandemic prepared us. Lots of time inside with only each other. Masking and hand-washing obsessively. Social distancing, even with our own kids, if there was the remote chance they were sick.

Luckily, just like the pandemic, we were able to slowly emerge from this isolation thanks to a white blood cell stimulating drug called Neulasta. This drug has to be taken within a specific time frame after each chemo session, so in my case weekly twenty-four to thirty-six hours after I finished treatment. My insurance required that I order it through their specialty pharmacy, and have the drug shipped to me in a refrigerated container. The first time that I needed the drug, the cancer center called in the order, and when I called to check on if it was being filled, I was told that everyone had left for the Christmas holiday. I vividly remember being in shock, wondering how in the hell a specialist pharmacy filling life-saving drugs for people like me could just close up shop three days before Christmas. The customer service person I was talking to started frantically searching to see if she could find it anywhere else. Could they ship it from New York? No, they are out of stock. Maybe the one in Kentucky has it. Nope, they are closed already too. Then in a Christmas miracle of sorts, she was able to find a random pharmacy in Ohio that was still open and still had the drug. I'd have it on my doorstep the next day.

Wouldn't you know it, they only sent me one dose. At this point, I was five days out from my next chemo session and would need to get more. But like any amazing medical insurance policy, I wasn't eligible to refill that prescription for a week. So I had to wait and repeat this process again. Of course this time, if you are tracking, we are running up against New Year's. So again, we did the interstate runaround of trying to find a pharmacy that was open and stocked. Eventually they were able to find it and get it to me. Thankfully, my care team was able to get me a month's worth of the drug this time so I wouldn't have to repeat this fun exercise on a weekly basis.

On cue, the drug worked. Even after the first dose, my white blood cell count was coming up and we could breathe a sigh of relief. It also meant that we could very cautiously start to emerge from isolation. The first time I left the house in weeks was to go to a friend's New Year's Day potluck. No germs there! I remember sitting in a corner outside, staying away from people. Masking up when I was inside, and not touching or eating anything that anyone else might have come in contact with before me. At this point, my hair had really started falling out and I was wearing a hat with a halo wig (halo wigs just go around the perimeter of your head and don't have a top, making them great to wear with a hat or head covering). People, especially those who didn't know I had cancer, had no idea. That is until I revealed in our friends' kitchen that I had no hair. Like my full wig, that was the only time I wore that halo thing. It was probably at that moment that I realized that the wig thing just wasn't for me, and I could be comfortable in my current "natural" state.

This was also a time where outdoor walks became everything. It was my chance to get outside and soak up a bit of winter sun and crisp air on my face. It also provided the exercise that was so important during and after treatment. Exercise not only helped with the fatigue, it literally helps to fight cancer, and keep it away. These walks were also an opportunity to connect in real life with my extended support system. Like my friend Jackie, who would dutifully put on her winter gear, and patiently walk with me around our neighborhood or hers, as I huffed and puffed to push my weak body to keep going.

As time went on, we continued to get more comfortable doing normal things out and about. The weather warmed, and seasonal flus and colds waned. What we quickly learned is that being a bald woman and wearing a mask is a pretty good signal to most people to keep their distance. This was especially use-ful at the mall where we learned one of the greatest benefits of having cancer is that you don't get harassed by those crazy mall kiosk people. Instead of running at you with their hand lotion, makeup, or whatever hair tool they are trying to sell, *they* run away from *you*. So next time you go to the mall and want to walk around in peace, just throw on a cancer head scarf, dust your face with pale powder, add a mask for extra emphasis, and boom, the mall as it should be.

Chapter Twelve

When My Grandma's Dog Had Cancer...

When you tell people you have cancer, inevitably people will try to be helpful and offer unsolicited advice. Typically, the advice doesn't stem from their own experience, or any scientific expertise, but comes from someone they know or something they read on the internet. It goes something like this:

"Megan, I'm so sorry you have cancer," says your concerned friend. "You'll be okay though. My cousin Sarah had breast cancer and she went on the alkaline diet, and now she is completely cured! You really should look into that. I think she even skipped chemo!"

"Huh…" you respond, not knowing what to do with this advice. And, honestly, WTF is the alkaline diet?

Your friend then says, "I'm praying for you."

You thank them and then run inside where you quickly Google "alkaline diet." At this point in cancer, even though it's only been a few weeks, you are an expert Googler. You've read every academic paper on your particular type of cancer, and the best course of treatment, etc. Nowhere in your extensive research did the alkaline diet come up, but hey, anything's worth a shot right?

Shockingly, there is no real scientific backing behind the alkaline diet itself, let alone the potential role it could play in fighting cancer. The idea behind the diet is that by consuming certain foods and beverages, you can ensure the proper pH of your body and counteract any acidic changes that may cause cancer and other diseases.

Turns out that changing the pH of your blood is a nearly impossible thing to do because your body has a shitload of mechanisms in place to prevent exactly that. Should you be able to make your blood more acidic or alkaline just by what you ate and drank, you'd be dead.

Then, there are the strangers (and there are many of them) who stop you on the street and suggest that you might be able to skip chemo altogether by going keto. It worked for someone they know!

Or the book you read where a lady used Pilates and a plant-based diet to beat her cancer. "Cancer hates cabbage!" she exclaimed. So I cut out red meat and gluten, only to find myself highly anemic. My oncologist insisted that I not change my diet while going through chemo. "Maybe after treatment, if you want."

There's even a renown Italian doctor who claims that he's unlocked the key to longevity through fasting. He recommends that cancer patients do his five-day fast during each round of their chemo to prepare their bodies, make the most of treatment, and reduce side effects. All at the low, low price of $200 a week for each fasting cycle.

So, yeah, okay, Ted from Home Depot, who noticed my lack of hair. I think I'll stick to the plan THE DOCTORS who are treating my cancer have come up with. It turns out they know a thing or two about keeping people alive. I appreciate your unsolicited advice, though!

Chapter Thirteen

Who Comes Up with This Shit?

I am obviously extremely grateful for the plan my doctors came up with, and the treatments that saved my life. Don't get me wrong. But I have to wonder how the fuck someone came up with chemotherapy?

"Hey, I have an idea," said Dr. Victor Frankenstein. "Let's see if we can pump someone full of toxic-ass chemicals that bring them to the brink of death, and hope that it mostly only kills the bad cells and not the patient.

And let's not just find one chemical that does this, let's come up with dozens of different ones that work in crazy ways to treat different types of cancers with all sorts of nasty side effects." It's mind-blowing.

My first twelve doses of weekly chemo were exhausting. Every Tuesday I would go in, have my labs done, see the doctor, then go through the multi-hour chemo process. The first set of chemo consisted of two chemo drugs, carboplatin and paclitaxel, which would be delivered sequentially. Immediately after treatment, I would be pretty okay that day and Wednesday thanks to the steroids they pumped me full of to stave off the nausea and other side effects. Then Thursday and Friday would hit, and I would progressively become dead to the world. Nauseated and exhausted, it was hard to function as a human yet alone as a mom or corporate worker bee. This is the time where I learned the beauty and art of napping. David had always made fun of me for not napping my entire adult life. In fact, I'm pretty sure he called me a "chump" multiple times for refusing to nap, just like a toddler. But in this cruel turn of events, I realized that napping was the only way that I was going to make it through and still be able to function at all.

Slowly, I would return to normal Saturday, Sunday, and Monday. We typically would be able to enjoy weekends together as a family so long as the activities weren't particularly active. Gone were weekends of hiking around Middle Tennessee and seeing the beautiful sites and waterfalls. Funnily enough, this is the time when we discovered what is now one of our favorite breweries in town, Yee-Haw Brewing Company. It was less so for the craft beer, and definitely not for the moonshine they also have, but more because they have a free arcade and a number of activities that keep the kids occupied like ping pong and basketball, while we could sit safely outside away from possible communicable diseases. And yes, I would drink a few beers even though I was on chemo. I still wonder if people thought it was weird that someone who was clearly chemo bald was having a beer. But whatever, it was just me again, employing Strategy #1 and trying to pretend everything was normal as much as possible. Then Tuesday would arrive and I would have to do it all over again. After the twelve rounds of this nerve-damaging chemo, where I got to trade frostbite for not having permanent nerve damage, I moved on to four rounds of what they call the Red Devil.

It's called this for a few reasons. First, it's color. It is bright red. Second, because of its nasty side effects. This one is evil. It produces noxious short-term side effects that make people feel like they are walking through the Valley of Death. It has been known to make fingernails and toenails fall out. In the long term, it can leave you with permanent heart damage.

But wait, there's more! The Red Devil is a vesicant—if it leaks onto your skin or escapes from the vein, it can cause burning and blistering. So, instead of being delivered via IV, a nurse in full hazmat gear has to hand-push it through a syringe over the course of ten to fifteen minutes. If she goes too fast, it will burn you from the inside out. And if it happens to spill during that time, a whole hazmat procedure must be followed.

While I got a break from the weekly chemo, this was rough. After going through the same routine of labs, doctor, and then treatment, I would be knocked out for a solid thirty-six hours after each of the Red Devil treatments. Partially from the drugs themselves and partially because of the additional meds they give you to keep the nausea away. Fun fact, did you know that a lot of the anti-nausea drugs are also anti-psychotics? I certainly didn't, but I'm sure the effects are twofold to keep cancer patients both from throwing up their guts and going crazy at the same time.

There were a lot of days in bed, and on our living room couch where I yearned to spend some normal moments with David and the kids. This was the point that my eyebrows and eyelashes fell out. That was traumatic in its own right, but luckily for me, I got to keep my finger and toenails and never got to experience a hazmat event. I'd still like to know how someone arrived at the idea of pumping this vesicant into people's veins and how it doesn't burn you from the inside out. And then how in the hell did they convince patients to take this medicine in the first place? That's Donald Trump-level marketing there.

Then there's radiation.

Hold my beer Dr. Frankenstein, *"I have another idea! What if we shoot radioactive lasers at people and see if that kills any microscopic cancer cells without killing the person at the same time?"* You read that right.

They make you a target by drawing marks on your skin where the lasers should hit. Again, lucky for me, these weren't actually tattoos like they used to do, but plain old Sharpies that I'm sure I was paying $300 a piece for. Then you lay down on a table in a very specific position with your arms above your head and you get transported into a giant $6 million machine that moves all around you shooting said lasers, supposedly not hitting any major organs, except perhaps, the top tip of the left lung. Sure, have at it. I always hated running anyway, so it's cool. You can have an eighth of my left lung.

Radiation will also give you the worst sunburn of your entire life. The doctors and radiation techs swore up and down that the radiation doesn't go all the way through your body, but I coincidentally had a really nice rash on my back exactly on the other side of where I was being radiated. But don't worry about it. It will save you. It's like Jesus, but better!

What will they come up with next?

Chapter Fourteen

Hospital Comment Card

January 18, 2023

Dear Breast Center,

It's a few weeks before Mardi Gras and the staff is trying to be festive by hanging beads up in the exam rooms. While the beads did brighten up the beige room a bit, they also gave me an idea that could truly make a difference for your patients!

On the off chance that people don't know how you earn beads in New Orleans, in NOLA, you earn beads by showing your breasts. Small breasts. Big breasts. Grandma's breasts. It doesn't matter. Everyone's a winner!

Megan Bannon

What if every visitor to the breast center who has to show their boobs (in other words, all of us) wins a set of Mardi Gras beads?

Not just the cancer patients (although we should get the really special ones) but all the people there for annual mammograms, the people with scan-xiety because they are on the other end of treatment (they should also get special ones too), really anyone who has to show off their tatas. Every time. Not just during Mardi Gras, all year round!

Think about the collection we frequent fliers would accumulate. It would bring a little fun to something that is often scary, anxiety-invoking, and, generally speaking, painful. I'm already dreaming about the collection of beads I could have at the end of this. It might make it all worth it. We'd all be winners.

Yours Truly,
Megan

Chapter Fifteen

The Grief Tourist

In the world of cancer, we like to talk about a certain type of person called a Grief Tourist. These are people that you know, but probably wouldn't consider yourself close to. They aren't invited to be part of your tribe because you know they will only do more damage to your cancer-ridden life. Usually they are distant relatives or long-forgotten friends who latch on to your tragedy to fuel their own ego. They have the special talent of somehow making your cancer about them. It's an unwelcome phenomenon that sadly, many cancer patients must deal with.

I was lucky. I didn't have a lot of these people. In fact, I had a pretty incredible tribe of people from near and far who rallied around me throughout my cancer journey.

But there was one…An ex-boyfriend. But not just any ex-boyfriend, *the* ex-boyfriend. The one my husband hates. The one my other ex-boyfriend even hates. He was that bad to me, and for me. I won't go into details, but there was cheating, deception, manipulation. Lifetime-movie-worthy behavior. Well, maybe not, he didn't murder me. Anyways, you get it.

When I finally was able to walk away for good—years after we had broken up—he couldn't stand it. Eventually, I had to cut him out of my life completely—no more texts, social media interactions, or emails.

So you can imagine that after not speaking to said person for over ten years, I was quite taken aback when out of the blue, *the* Grief Tourist emails.

This is a true story but to protect said Grief Tourist, and honestly, to not give him any more acknowledgement than he deserves, I've changed his name and a few identifying details. The emails you are about to read are basically as they were written, with some of my commentary in between.

From: Chad

Subject: Touching Base

Megan—I just learned about your diagnosis and current battle on LinkedIn, of all places. -

Please tell me things are looking good? And that you're ok? I know you have all the support in the world from family and friends, but if you need anything or if there's anything I can do, please let me know. I recently moved back to Chicago. Here if I can help in any way. Again—just hoping you're ok and will be ok.

Hope you and your family are well and that your health outlook is good and everyone else is happy and healthy.

Again, if you need anything or if I can ever help in any way, please let me know.

Sincerely,
Chad

I get this email, and I sit on it. WTF? So many thoughts running through my head.

LinkedIn? You really expect me to believe that you weren't just taking a peek at my profile to see where I'm at these days and happened to see my post about cancer?

Glad you are hoping I'll be okay since you never actually cared before.

By the way, I haven't lived in Chicago for several years and couldn't care less if you moved back or not.

And do you really think that out of all the people in the world, I would ask you for help?

I didn't tell my husband because I knew he would have an absolute freakout, which he did when he eventually found out. He's still mad about it, rightfully so. This guy was horrible to me and tried to get in between me and David for a long time. He was an unwelcome pest that took a long time to exterminate, so he certainly wasn't welcome back.

Caught off guard and upset that he showed back up in the middle of the emotional and physical rollercoaster I was on, I did consult two of my very good girlfriends who lived through the Chad ordeal with me and would have sound and objective advice on what to do.

"WTF? Tell him you are fine and to get back out of your life."

"Are you kidding me? What a narcissistic fuck."

"This guy...He just can't move on. Tell him you are glad that he's not your husband because he could never handle this."

I ponder whether he even deserves a response. Maybe I have David or a girlfriend write back and say

You Can't Take Them with You

that, sadly, "Megan passed away. Can you contribute to her funeral fund via Venmo?"

Ultimately, I respond as follows:

From: Megan

Re: Touching Base

Wow. I can't say this was an email I was expecting to receive.

Cancer sucks. Not exactly how I wanted to spend my 2023, but I'm gonna get through this and hopefully it's just a blip in the timeline.

I couldn't be luckier to have the team I have at Vanderbilt and the incredible support system ever.

The kids and David are doing well. They are troopers. We are all looking forward to a post-chemo celebration trip to the Dominican in May before more surgery and radiation.

Sounds like you've made it back to Chicago just in time for one of their amazing summers.

Thanks for checking in,
Megan

Days go by. I don't hear back. Maybe I successfully shut that down.

Then...

From: Chad

Re: Re: Touching Base

Megan—Sorry, I was in Hawaii for work this last week and then spent the weekend in San Francisco with family friends. Heading to the airport now for my flight back home.

I apologize—I didn't mean to blindside you with my email. The news really shook me. Glad to find that you're in good spirits, have a positive outlook and that you are well supported and receiving excellent care. No surprises on any of those fronts. Know you'll kick C's ass and beat this just like everything to else. While this certainly isn't one you sought out, you've never shied away from a challenge. I know you've got this.

I'm so happy to hear that David and the kids are rolling with it and hanging in there themselves. Sounds like everyone is doing well. I've been to the Dominican Republic many times, and you can't beat the DR in the spring. Loved it when I went last year. Glad you all have something special to look forward to.

Landed back in Chicago early fall. It's been great. Validating after being away for four years. Good to be home and to know you're home.

I hope things continue to go well for you. As you said, hopefully just a blip. Sending positive energy your way and hoping to hear positive updates in the future. If you or the fam ever need anything, please don't hesitate to reach out.

Sincerely,
Chad

Ah, there it is. I knew it was coming. This had nothing to do with me at all. He truly doesn't care but would show up heartbroken at my funeral if I died. "I was just emailing with her last week," he'd say as he wiped away a tear.

And he just couldn't resist the not-so-humble brag of his trips to Hawaii, San Francisco, and the Dominican Republic. Hey dude, I'm going through chemo and looking forward to a celebration trip with my family. Don't need your travelog.

Oh, sorry that *my* cancer diagnosis shook *you*. Glad you started caring now that I might die.

(End Communication)

Chapter Sixteen

Better Update My Will!

Let me take you back to 2010, when David and I got married. After our wedding, we took an amazing honeymoon trip to Spain. I can't quite recall how my husband came across it, but somehow he got his hands on a KISS (yes the seventies rock band with the black and white face paint) throw blanket. My mom dared him to put it on me while I was sleeping on the plane ride over and capture a picture. Of course he did it. A picture-perfect start to our marriage.

Skip ahead twelve years to 2022. When I was diagnosed with cancer, I instantly became acutely aware of my mortality, and it was hard not to think that I might actually die. One of the very first questions I asked was if we were still paying for my life insurance policy.

Honestly, thank goodness we had adulted a few years before and had gotten those policies. It was helpful to know that if I did die, I wouldn't leave my family in financial ruin.

For a while in the beginning of this whole ordeal, I thought that I was for sure going to die. I had a very aggressive form of cancer that up until very recently didn't have great prognoses. But once I started chemo and could feel my tumor shrinking, I slowly became less panicked about death and started to realize that maybe, just maybe, I would come out alive on the other side.

One day, David and I were taking a walk, as you do when hanging out with someone with cancer, one of us made a joke about death. Then he told me that if I died, he was going to put me in a KISS-themed casket. Not only do I not ever want to be in a casket, the thought of spending my eternal life in a KISS-themed one was enough motivation to keep me alive. It was at that moment that I realized that I needed to update my will to be VERY SPECIFIC so David couldn't use this as an opportunity to get the last joke.

The next day, I started texting with one of my very good friends who had been on the cancer journey eighteen months longer than I had. We started laughing about the idea of a KISS-themed casket, and that led to the most incredible funeral planning session you could imagine. Here's the text chain (edited for clarity):

I might need to update my will
since David has threatened things
like a KISS themed casket…

HAHAHA
Perfect

If I die, I want everyone to go to an
all inclusive on a beach and just
get wasted & have a blast while
they cry about me.

That's the Irish way, ya know
Get drunk, Dance, talk about
us And how great I was

Exactly

LOL

I also want to create my own
playlist

YES I think about that all the
time! I might write it down

LOTS of Tupac

Of course, for you

Songs I know people hate and
I love but they have to listen
because it was my dying wish

HAHAHAHAHA
You're a genius. I used to say
I wanted to be strung up in a
harness and fly down into my
casket as a special entrance

You'd give some old person a
heart attack

To the tune of the Final
Countdown. I'm going for cre-
mation though so that's out of
the cards

Same. Although now I'm reading
about these green burials and I'm
intrigued

You Can't Take Them with You

OMG me too...
the composting one

Yes!

Ashes to ashes, dust to dust

My dad and sis have huge
gardens... would it be weird to
eat a salad fueled by me??

Yes

LOL

Just being honest

Tastes like Anni

They'd cry at every bite of carrot

LOL
Delicious

I have to stop laughing. I have to
go into a meeting.

• • •

I lost this friend.

She didn't fly into her casket from the rafters to the tune of "The Final Countdown." She didn't have a casket. She did, however, have a lovely celebration of life that took me and David to Tucson, Arizona, less than a week after I had finished my active cancer treatment. A place we never would have gone to without her. There we got to see the landscape of the Southwest, including the most amazing cacti we had ever seen. We were having a bit of a double rainbow moment as we took it all in, and we started our journey of processing what had happened over the last nine months, including losing two friends in the process.

She was a great friend and rock for me during my cancer treatment. I wouldn't miss the opportunity to stand up at her celebration and say a few words, so I retold a story that I hoped would lift everyone's spirits. While this has nothing to do with cancer (besides us both having it after this happened) it is a story worth retelling.

Chapter Seventeen

Annicka Gets Married

Let's go back about four years. My dear friend Annika is getting married in Chicago on a boat. It's a picture-perfect summer day near the river. My husband and I are excited to celebrate our friend and, frankly, have some time away from our two- and five-year-old kids. We decided to go early and enjoy a glass or two of wine by the river before making our way to the boat. I am the neurotic type who reads invitations one hundred times, makes sure I know the details intimately, and insists on being places extra early. Especially when there's a boat involved.

This time, however, we got a little lost in the wine and the beautiful weather and I looked down and realized that boat boarding time was quickly approaching.

It was time to go. So we dart the block or two down the river path to the boat dock and the boat is pulling away as we approach.

Frantically, we go running up to the boat. "IS THIS THE WEDDING?"

Random boat guy says, "yes!"

"For Annicka and Jef?" I yell.

"Yes!"

Then there's a bit of a flurry while they contact the captain. Good news, he's able to pull back up to the dock and we are allowed to board.

The moment we stepped on the boat, we knew that something was off. It just didn't feel right.

Then we get upstairs where all the guests are waiting. I don't recognize a single person. I figured I would see her sister (her twin, not hard to spot). Or her parents, who I thought I would recognize. I didn't see them, but I noticed that about half the guests look Hispanic. My friend isn't Hispanic, but I've never met her fiancé.

We also seem severely under-dressed for this boat. My husband is in shorts and every other man is wearing a full suit. This wasn't right. Annicka and Jef had specifically told people to come in whatever they were comfortable in. They were not the *super formal men in suits even though it's ninety degrees out* types.

I frantically started texting my friend, fully understanding that she was likely getting ready for her wedding and probably not looking at her phone. To my complete surprise, she actually responds, "OMG, I'm not sure but I think you are on the wrong boat." Just then, the groom shows up, and the bride (not Annika) starts walking down the aisle.

Confirmed. We are on the wrong wedding boat.

I am mortified. This is my worst nightmare. As someone with general social anxiety, I really don't like new situations and people I don't know. Not to mention the absolute faux pas of being at the wrong wedding. I am freaking out. As usual, my husband is laughing. He's trying to convince me that we should just crash the whole thing. "What a story," he says!

Nope. Not my story. So as soon as the ceremony is over, I march us straight to the first official person and explain what has happened. They sit us near the captain, away from the guests who are now all on the lower deck of the boat, and we wait. Luckily, the reverend who had performed the marriage rites was not staying for the reception, so they were heading to the dock to drop him (and us) off.

As we are headed back, we see the right wedding boat go by just as my friend and her almost-husband are saying their vows. We wave frantically, so sad to miss this momentous event. David even captured a picture of them saying their vows from the vantage point of the wrong boat.

After I told this story at Annika's funeral, so many people who did not miss the boat came up to us. Turns out, word traveled fast on the boat about our misadventure. We were famous. While I hate that we missed her wedding, I love that we had this story to retell and bring laughter and light to those she loved.

Luckily for us, her celebration of life was in land-locked Tucson, so we couldn't miss the boat this time.

Chapter Eighteen

The Worst Part of Cancer

Growing up, I wasn't really a girly-girl. I wouldn't say I was a tomboy either. I was just indifferent to pink and frills. I didn't lust after dresses and dolls. I'm not sure I even combed my hair, yet alone styled it. This made for some great school pictures (thanks Mom and Dad!).

To this day, I don't know how to French braid, much to the chagrin of my girly-girl daughter. In fact, my husband and I are probably on par for our skills in doing our daughter's hair—he might even be better.

This indifference also applied to things like my eyebrows and makeup. I think I got my eyebrows threaded a few times in college at the urge of my roommate, Kim. You could also put me in the category of folks who over-plucked in the nineties and, therefore, had relatively thin eyebrows (not pencil-thin). But this never bothered me. I was more grateful for not having bushy brows to deal with because I wouldn't know where to start.

As for makeup, I once read in a Cindy Crawford makeup book my Aunt Sue gave me when I was twelve that if you take more than five minutes to put makeup on in the morning, you are taking too long. I took that to heart. This laissez-faire approach to beauty served me well for the first thirty-eight or so years of my life. Then I got cancer.

It's common knowledge that people going through chemo often lose their hair. In theory, that's easy to deal with. You can just put a wig on it! Just don't let your eight-year-old pick out said wig. I hadn't really thought about it before, but it makes sense that hair loss wouldn't be limited to their heads. How nice, no shaving my underarms, legs or best of all, the bikini area. But one thing I had never thought about was that it also applies to eyebrows and eyelashes.

This was by far the worst part about cancer (it wasn't, but for the sake of drama, just play along with me). I think I handled being bald with ease minus the Kosher wig mistake. It was expected, and I leaned in with various hats and headwear. But when I started the Red Devil and my eyelashes and eyebrows started to fall out, my whole life flashed before my eyes. What had I been doing all these years? How did I not realize that a face without eyebrows is just an emoji? Worse, I was wholly unprepared to deal with this. I was lost.

So I did what any sane adult woman would do, and I asked a couple of twelve-year-old girls for advice. Turns out, twelve-year-olds know more about everything than anyone because they have this thing called TikTok. Their generation has even recently been deemed "Sephora girls" because of how much they are driving the thriving beauty economy. "Did you know that there are temporary tattoo eyebrows that you can get on Amazon?", they immediately answered.

Yes, the same type of temporary tattoos that kids put all over their bodies. Same application method as well, a wet paper towel, just of eyebrows of various styles instead of the princess-themed ones my five-year-old puts on her wrist. I did not know that this was a thing. I ordered them and thanks to Amazon they were on my doorstep the next day. It changed my life. Perhaps I would never go back to actual eyebrows because my tattoo eyebrows were to die for. Perfect in every way. Honestly, when they were on, you couldn't tell that they were fake.

Perfect, that was, until my actual eyebrows started growing back and the tattoos would no longer stick to my face. Another plan gone to shit. Thanks cancer. I would have to deal with yet another awkward phase of my life and let my brows grow in enough that I could do the second twelve-year-old's suggestion: get them tinted. Tinted? What the fuck does that mean? It means that they temporarily dye the skin under your eyebrows along with the baby eyebrow hairs, to make them look fuller and have more shape. Little old me had no idea that was a thing, but I'm a convert and may never go back.

Now let's talk about those eyelashes: you really miss them when they're gone. Eyes without eyelashes are very obvious. I felt extremely self-conscious about this part of my appearance. My face and eyes are a focal point on my work Zoom calls. I already have no hair and fake eyebrows, adding a lack of eyelashes to the mix was the tipping point. To have some sense of power over the situation, I bought a number of false eyelash solutions. Ones you put on with glue. Ones that are magnetic. Ones with adhesive so you just stick them on.

Every time I attempted to put one on, I feared for my eyeballs. It was not pretty. I had no experience, no coordination, and there was a real chance I was going to poke an eyeball out or glue my eyelids together. How sad would that be? Megan survived cancer, but lost an eyeball because she's vain and wanted eyelashes…

I eventually gave up.

Cancer is hard, but being eyelash- and eyebrow-less is the hardest. Take it from the person who looked like the main character in the movie *Powder*, a hairless albino, for about twelve weeks. Although unlike in the movie, I was lacking the powers of telepathy and the ability to control lightning. At least I didn't have to worry about thunderstorms.

Chapter Nineteen

Let's take a Menopause

Do you know what's really unfair about going through cancer in your thirties? Menopause.

You know what's extra unfair about going through menopause during cancer treatment? It's temporary.

That's right. Not only did I get to go through all the hot flashes, night sweats, and mood swings of menopause while dealing with all the other cancer shit, I'll get to do it all over again when I'm actually going through menopause.

It's one of those things they don't really mention until it's happening. They might mention that your periods could stop while you are going through chemo. What they don't tell you is that you will go through the motions of menopause. You've seen all the commercials, it's not fun. Hot flashes that hit all the time, waking me up in a pool of sweat, or breaking out when I'm on a Zoom call with my boss. Not a great look. Or the mood swings that make a frustrating moment with kids, like when they won't just get their damn shoes on and get out of the house, even more frustrating. It wasn't pretty behavior in those moments.

So I'm cool, at least until the hot flashes start, with this being permanent. I'm totally done having kids. I would really love to never have a period again. Are you sure we can't just somehow make this permanent while we're here? Just call it another little fringe benefit of cancer?

No?

Cool.

Chapter Twenty

Jesus

When you start telling people you have cancer, a common response is that someone will start praying for you, and so will their family. Maybe even their prayer group or whole church! And while I no longer consider myself a religious person, I was 100% for this. The truth is, any positivity in the universe was and still is welcome. If that came in the form of prayer, bring it on.

Also, if I'm totally honest, I haven't completely given up on the idea that there is a God and an afterlife. As I was thinking about the very real possibility of facing death, it also crossed my mind that it might not be a bad idea to hedge my bets a bit and start talking to God myself. You know, just in case . . . I mean, either way it's win-win, right? I die and there's no God—I'll never know. I die and there is a God—then maybe, just maybe—I'll make the cut and Saint Peter will let me pass through the pearly gates into heaven. I opened my mind to the possibility in a way I hadn't for a long time, and then one day that sign showed up on my doorstep.

During my bout with cancer, I was showered with love from near and far. Care packages, gifts, notes, texts, and just amazing amounts of love. It was incredible and made me realize how many people out there were rooting for me. Then one day, this oddly decorated box shows up. It's got a turtle on the outside and says, "you turtlely got this!"

I'm thinking, "This is fun!"

I open the box and inside I find the following:

- A bright green and dark green fleece blanket.
- A bright green and dark green knit hat.
- A Bible.
- A care kit with essentials, such as toothpaste and lotion.
- A seat belt cushion to protect my chemo port from the seatbelt.

All these things are very thoughtful gifts for a cancer patient, but I am SO confused. Who could have sent this? Then I get to the cards. Not one card, but many. All these people who are praying for me. Not one of them is someone I know. Notes, words of encouragement, Bible verses. And a note that explains that this care package was sent anonymously through a certain religious organization in Indiana.

I start dying with laughter. What crazy friend would send me this? No one super close to me is that religious. Maybe it was sent as a joke? I asked around. Made some educated guesses, but no one revealed who the sender was. Look, it was thoughtful. But who wanted me to dress like a Ninja Turtle when I went to chemo? Do they sincerely believe that this *is* what Jesus would have wanted?

Actually, the more I thought about it, the more I realized that the God I believe in would 100% want me to go to chemo looking like a Ninja Turtle. Well played, God. Well played.

Still, we had no idea who sent it. We had some guesses, but nothing definitive.

• • •

Now skip ahead a month or so, and I get a piece of mail from the same organization. I open it up and on the front there is a very cute little drawing of an elephant, clearly colored in by a child.

On the front it says, "How do you stop an elephant from charging?"

Open it up and it says, "Take away his credit cards!"

Then it reads:

Dear Friend…

Wishing you peace and love!

Trust in the LORD with all your heart and lean not on your own understanding.

-Proverbs 3:5

Name: Michael _

Age: 52

Fifty-two?!? A grown man has sent me a page out of a coloring book with a children's joke? Michael, whoever you are, I appreciate your kind words and wishes. But dude, leave the crayons to the kindergartners and forward your address so I can send you an adult coloring book; I have a few I'm not using.

The notes continued to come monthly, and I honestly looked forward to them. Complete strangers sending me cute colorings and corny jokes. Jesus believer or not, religious or not, they brought a smile to my face. Random people, who I didn't even know, were taking the time and effort to put goodwill into the world for me. And that's the type of love and laughter that kept me going.

Chapter Twenty-one

Chemo Bell, You Tease!

Twenty-four long weeks of chemo were coming to a close. I don't know what the origins of the tradition are, but at the end of chemo there is a bell that you ring to signal that this part of your journey is over. My best friend, Kim, had flown in for the event, and it was going to be a big deal. Knowing that I would be knocked out by the Red Devil on the actual day of chemo, Grandma babysat the kids so David, Kim, and I could go out to a celebratory dinner the night before. I even had a glass of wine. Something I typically would not do the day before chemo.

The day I had waited six months for was finally here. Chemo is not something you look forward to, but I was so excited for this stage of treatment to be over that

I could barely sleep the night before in anticipation. I made a big thank-you basket of snacks for the nurses and added a little thank you note. My way of cementing myself as the best cancer patient ever, even long after my visits to the infusion center were over.

> Dear Infusion Nurses,
>
> Thank you so much for taking such great care of me over the last 24 weeks. You are life savers.
>
> No offense, but I hope I never see you again.
>
> Love,
> Megan

Smug in thinking I was so clever and nice at the same time, David, Kim, and I excitedly rolled up to the infusion center. As always, I checked in and had labs done, then went to see my oncologist. David and I went in together, leaving Kim out in the waiting area.

My oncologist (who I love) had her usual questions. She did an exam and checked my labs. Then she dropped a bomb. While I might be done with chemo, I had nine more rounds of immunotherapy to complete. This meant being back at the infusion center every three weeks for the next six months. What I thought would be ending in May wouldn't be over until December.

While immunotherapy has a lot fewer side effects than chemo and doesn't make you nauseated or make your hair fall out, this was devastating. I was nowhere near being done. We held it together and walked out of the oncologist's office to where Kim was waiting. I completely lost it. Through my tears, I said to her, "Dammit, I jinxed myself with that damn note to the nurses!"

We took our basket of goodies and the note I should never have written down the hall so I could check in for chemo. Once we were all settled in my room, my assigned nurse came in to get started. Of course, it was my least favorite infusion nurse. It's not that she was mean, or anything, she just lacked personality. She never laughed at my jokes or recited rap lyrics with me. Never preemptively offered the Ativan, even though she had to know at this point I was going to ask for it. Clearly she had no interest in buying into my campaign to be her favorite patient. With the day going the way it was, I deserved her.

So, of course, her first question was, "Are you going to ring the bell?"

I burst into tears again.

A few minutes later, once the pre-meds were going and I was being rocked into my chemo stupor, I said yes. I truly was excited to be done with the chemo and especially the Red Devil bit of all of this, but I couldn't help feeling that the bell ringing was totally anti-climactic. I had nine more sessions of immunotherapy ahead of me, a double mastectomy in a month, and six weeks of radiation after that. And depending on the outcome of the surgery, if they found residual cancer, I could have another round of chemo.

Yeah, damn right I'll ring that bell.

I'd give the bell-ringing experience a two out of five stars. I remember thinking I should take my treat basket back from the nurses. Fortunately, David and Kim were not high out of their minds from anti-nausea drugs and were one step ahead of me. When I turned to go back in the door, they knew exactly what I was doing and carried me off into my chemo sunset.

Chapter Twenty-two

Selling My Soul for Passports

There was about a month break between the end of chemo and my double mastectomy surgery. Given the last six months of hell our whole family had gone through, we decided to treat ourselves to an all-inclusive vacation in the Caribbean.

This trip hadn't exactly been on our radar, because there were a lot of unknowns in our lives. When we realized that this window was going to be our only viable one for a family trip, we booked it. From that moment on, I lived for it. For the past almost six months, I had been living in isolation and feeling terrible. Imagine the deepest of pandemic days, that was my life. Masks, no crowds. Generally no fun. When your immune system is shot, there's no fun. And my family was along for this not-at-all-fun ride. This window between chemo and surgery meant everything for all of us. It was a chance for us to unwind and start to work through everything we had all gone through. A reset before the next phases of treatment started. We had about twelve weeks until the trip. We thought there was plenty of time to get our older kid's passport renewed and get the younger one her first one. Boy, were we wrong!

Unfortunately for us, apparently, everyone in the United States had the same idea. For kids, you have to go to a passport office in person with both parents. The earliest we could get an appointment was a month away. That gave us about eight weeks of buffer to get the passports back, which, with expedited service, should have been plenty of time. Except it wasn't.

The very day we went to our appointment at the post office downtown, the State Department had notified all passport processing locations that the "expedited" service was backed up, and was now taking seven to nine weeks. We had eight.

We got the applications in, and we waited. I wouldn't say "waited patiently," because I became a daily visitor to the passport status website to see if anything had changed. For the first time in six months, I had a new obsession that wasn't MyChart. The weeks ticked by, and nothing happened. Then we were two weeks out and we still didn't have passports. I had thought their estimates were an under-promise for an over-delivery. Again, I was wrong.

So I did what any logical adult would do: I consulted social media. I put out a call for help, asking if anyone had a connection in the U.S. State Department, particularly in the Passports Office. While no one came forward, I did get some helpful advice. Either make an appointment for same-day service at one of the twenty main passport offices across the country or and whatever it takes to get there and get it done. Our closest main office was in Atlanta, a three-hour drive away. Remember: four of us, in person.

The second option was more reasonable: write your senators and ask for their help. I happen to live in a ruby red state. And as you've probably gathered from some of my other views, I'm not exactly aligned with far-right perspectives. This meant I would have to suck it up and ask someone I despise for help. I sold my soul for a trip to the Dominican Republic.

This is when having cancer comes in handy. David, who doesn't mind talking to people on the phone, called her office and played the cancer card. Within an hour, he had a form to fill out with the specifics of our request. That was a Monday.

By Tuesday, the status of our kids' passport applications had been updated to "processing." By Thursday, we had the passports in hand.

It worked. Praise my Ninja Turtle-loving God!

You may think that your elected representatives are useless, but regardless of their political views, know that if your passport application gets held up, they can do something for you that has a real-life impact—even if it means selling your soul in the process.

Chapter Twenty-three

How to Explain Mastectomy to Kids

"Mommy, when are you getting your boobs cut off?"

It was not exactly the question I was expecting from my five-year-old during school drop-off on a typical Monday morning, but I guess I had it coming.

At this point, we were about six months into my cancer journey. I was finishing chemo, and the next step was a double mastectomy. Just like we had handled the rest of this ordeal, we were pretty straightforward with our kids about what was going on.

First point of order: what do we call *them*? Breasts? Boobs? Tatas? Let's just go with "boobs," no need to get formal about this.

One night my husband and I sat them down and explained mastectomy in the most kid friendly way we could devise. "Now that I'm finishing chemo and my tumor is nearly gone, they are going to cut off my boobs just to make sure that they get all the cancer, and it doesn't come back."

We told them that Mommy will be functioning with T-Rex arms for about two weeks, and we'd need their extra help during that time since I won't be able to reach above my head.

Not knowing what to expect, we got a very practical set of questions from them.

"Would it hurt?"

"No, probably not, but they will make sure that I have medicine to be comfortable."

"How long will you be in the hospital?"

"Just a few days, and Grandma will be here to help while I'm gone."

They seemed pretty understanding about the situation and were satisfied with our answers. Another parenting high-five as we appeared to have successfully navigated a possibly confusing and complicated conversation with ease. Personally, I was grappling with what losing my boobs meant for my identity. Did this make me less feminine or less of a woman? What would it be like to have a flat chest and scars for at least six to twelve months? Would I be less attractive as a result of this? They didn't have any of these worries and it seemingly made perfect sense to my kids. They were happy to get back to playing Roblox and watching *Frozen*. Everything was normal.

What I didn't expect was the follow-up questions the next day after they'd had the chance to process a bit more.

"What do they *do* with them after they cut them off?"

Before I could even start to tackle that question, he fired off his next question excitedly.

"Could we put them in the compost!?"

Deep breath. "No. Sadly, you can't take them with you. And even if you could, they probably wouldn't make great backyard composting material."

Chapter Twenty-four

Getting my Boobs Cut Off

A month after chemo ended it was time for my double mastectomy. Given the aggressiveness of my cancer, my doctors wanted to give my body enough time to heal from chemo so that my body would be able to recover from surgery, but not enough time to let any cancer cells take hold again. So they moved quickly.

My mom came in to help for a few weeks and we sent the kids off to summer camp that week, so we had one less logistic to deal with for a few days. I prepared similarly to chemo by doing as much advanced preparation as possible. This included simple things like a fancy lip moisturizing mask, recommended by a friend who had her mastectomy a few months before, and said she woke up with super dry lips. She also recommended a

$300 pillow system that would help make sleep more comfortable after surgery. Imagine an adult-sized version of the Dock-A-Tot, the cult sleeper system for infants. It's a large U-shaped pillow that you lay in with wedges to help elevate your torso and legs. As someone who has never been able to sleep on their back, this was worth the investment if it meant I would be comfortable and be able to sleep while I healed. (I have since recommended this system to two other friends.)

My preparation also included a number of really fucking ugly shirts that had pockets to put my drains in. When you have a mastectomy, your body tries to send fluid and such to help fill and heal the space that was there. That fluid doesn't have anywhere to go anymore, so it can build up if they don't put drains in to help remove it. For a number of weeks after surgery you wear these grenade-sized drains with tubes coming out of holes they've left for drainage, one on each side. These have to be flushed multiple times a day, and the liquid measured and logged to bring into the doctor's office on checkups. Once the drainage slows enough, they can take them out. The pockets on the shirts give you a place to put those while you try to function as a human being. Seriously though, someone needs to make some more fashionable options for breast cancer patients so we don't look like we've just broken out of jail.

The day of my mastectomy wasn't that different from any other day in the life of a cancer patient. We rolled up to the hospital early in the morning. I didn't quite know where we were supposed to go, but David, having taken me here for my chemo port insertion, knew exactly what to do. We checked into the surgery center and a bit later were taken back to get prepped for surgery. This process takes about two hours. During that time, they put me in this amazing lavender-colored paper gown with these lovely holes for connecting a vacuum-sized hose that then blows air, hot or cold depending on what you need, into the gown. It puffs up and makes you look like Violet Beauregard from *Willy Wonka and the Chocolate Factory* when she balloons up like a blueberry. Each of the doctors parades around to your room one by one to discuss the plan. What the anesthesiologist's plan is. What the supervising nurse will be doing. The surgeon herself is the last one. They give me a pregnancy test, even though my tubes are tied, I have an IUD, and I've gone through chemo-induced menopause, just in case. Good news, I'm not pregnant! Then I'm good to go. Final kisses to

David, and I'm off to the operating room for the next few hours.

The surgery went smoothly. They did not compost my boobs. I spent the next two nights in the hospital recovering and learning how to care for myself at home. Usually, this would have only been one night, but I had some worrisome bleeding that they wanted to keep an eye on for an extra night.

With my chest bound tightly and stuffed with gauze, I was sent home to continue recovering over the next four to six weeks. What they didn't tell me until I was leaving the hospital is that I would not be allowed to shower until the drains came out. Two or three weeks without a shower. Not, no baths or swimming pools, but also no shower water hitting my drains. As a daily shower-er, this was quite possibly the longest few weeks of my life. While I became accustomed to my daily sponge bath, and body wipes became my best friend, I swear you could still smell me from miles around. Needless to say, I was very motivated to get those drains out so I could have the best shower of my life.

The drains came out about two weeks after my surgery, and I was slowly able to return to normal life. Although, they made me wait ANOTHER 24 HOURS to shower after they came out. While I *technically* wasn't allowed to lift my arms above my head for however many weeks, I disobeyed orders and did it anyways while my mom yelled at me for doing so. I went to a number of physical therapy sessions to work on getting my full range of motion back. This happened pretty quickly. I attribute it to continuing to exercise, even if only lightly, and doing Pilates throughout my treatment and in preparation for my surgery. After about three weeks I was bored to tears and wanted to get back to work and normal life. Sitting around the house watching Netflix all day is fun for only so long. Cancer treatment phase two was over, and I had about eight weeks before my final phase of treatment, radiation, was due to start.

Chapter Twenty-five

Survivors Guilt

Sometime in the summer, after chemo and my mastectomy, but before radiation started, we were out at a music and beer event by the river. This is a summer-long ritual on Fridays in East Nashville where we lived. It's always a lovely evening where we run into tons of friends from school and the neighborhood. At this point, my hair was starting to grow back. The side effects from chemo were starting to become a memory, and I was looking healthier and happier than I'd been in a long time. They found no evidence of cancer when they inspected my tissue after my double mastectomy and felt confident that they had gotten anything that was lingering in my lymph nodes as well. This was as good as things get when you have triple-negative breast cancer. Radiation at this point was insurance to kill any leftover microscopic cancer cells to reduce the risk of recurrence.

This particular day, I happened to spot a dad, Doug, we knew from our kids' previous school. His daughter was in my daughter's class a few years before, and our daughters did dance together at one point. We hadn't seen him in a while, and I'm not sure he even knew that I had cancer. Why this mattered was that he had lost his wife to cancer the day before Thanksgiving two years before. The year our daughters were in the same class together.

We didn't really know him and his wife before it happened. We had some interactions during drop off and pick up but were not aware that she had cancer. When the school notified the class that Everly's mom had died, we signed up for the Meal Train, of course. Our spot was actually a few months later, and at this point, David had befriended Doug. He had gotten to talking to him about everything and Doug had mentioned that he was getting a little tired of the dropped-off meals, and even the takeout. So we asked what would be most helpful and ended up giving him a gift card for a grocery store, so he and Everly could be in more control of what they ate.

We also learned in this time that how she died came on quite suddenly and was very traumatic. She had cervical cancer and had been battling the disease for three years. At some point, things were seemingly looking up and she was getting stronger, but then, as cancer too often does, it came back. One night Cathy and Doug were having a campfire with friends. Cathy had stayed up most of the night, but by the end was extremely tired and knew that something was off. They went to the emergency room. She was examined and then sent home. Still not feeling great, she went back in on Monday and they did a CT scan where they found small blood clots in her lungs. She ended up staying in the hospital until Wednesday, the day before Thanksgiving. They had hoped she could make it home in time for the holiday, and their daughter Everly was sleeping over with friends. She did get released that night, but it was a bit late, so they decided to leave Everly where she was. They ordered takeout and watched a movie. Cathy went up to bed, but that's when trouble started. Doug called 911. The paramedics took her away. She didn't even make it to the hospital. Cancer, you fucking asshole.

• • •

Here I am, alive, seemingly on the upside of cancer. I'm having a beer and a good time with friends, and when I see Doug, I panic. This is less than two years since his wife died of cancer. He doesn't know that I have cancer. Is he going to get really sad when he sees my bald head? Why am I alive, and she's not? Why am I projecting all my emotions at this moment? I can't imagine my kids having to process my death. It all rushes in and I am overwhelmed by my own emotions. Perhaps Strategy #1 has been working a little too well.

I turn and walk in the opposite direction. This was a good excuse to check on the kids anyway. When I walk back, of course David is talking to Doug. When he sees me, he immediately says, "David told me what's going on. I'm so glad you are doing well." I smile and am instantly calmed by his calm. Then we just start talking like normal adults. Eventually, I told him during this encounter, or maybe it was the next time we saw him, that I was writing a book all about the comedic outtakes of my cancer journey. Like most people I tell that to, he really likes the idea and says he could write a guest chapter about one of the darkest comedy moments he had in his experience.

As you can imagine, the night his wife died, it was sudden. It was tragic. He was in shock. It was the day before Thanksgiving. While most families are getting ready to cook a huge meal and deal with family drama, he's figuring out what you do when your wife dies. There's no real manual for this, so I'm sure the next steps were absolutely paralyzing. He's dealing with medical staff. Trying to say his own goodbyes. Calling the people who needed to be called. He's in the room with his wife's then-lifeless body and a nurse keeps coming in and asking him which funeral home she's going to. He says, "I don't know yet."

Yet, she persists and keeps coming in every thirty minutes or so to ask him. "We really need to move her body," she says.

"I still haven't figured it out. It's the middle of the night. Can you please give me a little bit of time," he begs.

She leaves, and then like clockwork comes back and looks at him with that, "*I know you know what I'm going to ask you*" look.

Finally he shouts, "I'm waiting for the Black Friday sales, okay?"

Well that shut her up. In horror, she left the room. Doug didn't see that nurse again.

Chapter Twenty-six

My Radiation Friends

I didn't get to make chemo friends like some people do. I was lucky enough to be at a place where I got a private room for my infusions. But that all changed when I started radiation.

For those lucky folks who haven't been through radiation, it is typically a four- to six-week-long extravaganza where you go in at the same time every day Monday through Friday for a quick boost of nuclear energy. What I didn't know before cancer but learned is that radiation is a pretty quick process. On most days I would be in and out of the machine in about 10 minutes, making the commute to and from the hospital the longest part of those days. Don't take that to mean that radiation is easy, however. It's a total slog, and it might have been harder than chemo. While the side effects are less dramatic in the way of nausea, it can really burn your skin and the fatigue is not to be trifled with.

They try to schedule your appointments at the same time every day. In my case, I was there early every morning so I could get on with my workday afterward. As you can imagine, you start to see the same people day-to-day because they are on the same schedule as you, even if they are getting treated for a different cancer. Some I just passed in the hallway on a regular basis, some I just listened to while in the waiting room, and one became my temporary friend.

There was another young woman with breast cancer. We both had the post-chemo, no-boob, baby-hair-growth look going for us, so it was easy to tell. Her appointment time was right before mine, so she would be leaving as I was sitting in the waiting area to get started. We never spoke, but we knew, so there was always a smile and a nod. We were by far the youngest people in the radiation waiting room. Sisters united in a shared experience.

Then there was my favorite couple who I loved to listen to in the waiting room. The gentleman had cancer, and his wife came with him every day for the hour-and-a-half drive each way. One day, I overheard another friendly patient ask them why they weren't taking advantage of the housing that the hospital provides for people coming from afar. To which they responded that you had to be vaccinated and boosted for COVID to qualify. The audacity! It didn't stop there though; it devolved into a conversation about a young woman they knew who got cancer a few months after getting vaccinated. They were certain the two were related. No way were they going to be guinea pigs for the government and pharmaceutical companies. They would take no part in having that sweet 5G running through their veins.

Don't get me wrong, I love a good conspiracy theory. I just found it ironic that they were sitting in a world-class medical institution, letting the doctors shoot radioactive lasers at their body, but unwilling to take a vaccine that the same doctors were recommending. Not to mention that he was immunocompromised, and this vaccine could save his life if he did get COVID. Clearly, the doctors were in on the conspiracy too.

Then there was my friend Tom. After seeing each other for a few days and some friendly "good mornings," we got to talking. Turns out that this was Tom's second time going through radiation because he had a different type of cancer nine years before. This time, he was doing radiation and chemo at the same time. It was really taking it out of him. He could barely speak. Every time I saw him, he would call me Superwoman, as if what I was going through was more incredible than the journey he had already been on and was on again.

I took myself to all my radiation sessions except for the last one. The sessions were quick and didn't have the same impact on me as chemo did. There was no reason I needed to drag David along for the six-week daily trek. However, I did bring David to the last session. That day, I was going to ring the bell once and for all. Unlike when I did it with chemo, this time I was actually done. It was the end of my active treatment.

That day, David got to meet Tom, a person I had told him about at home. On cue, Tom went on and on about how I was so amazing and strong, and then he called me Superwoman for the last time. I'll probably never see Tom again and I'll never know if he made it through his second slog. But I'll never forget how he brightened up a tough period for me on a daily basis.

Chapter Twenty-seven

Lobster Rolls

One of the people we began to recognize week after week during chemo, was a shockingly young woman who couldn't have been older than twenty-one. At first, we weren't sure if she was the one going through treatment or if it was her mother. Eventually, when we noticed that the young woman's hair changed drastically from week to week. She was wearing wigs. It had to be her.

After a few weeks of observing her in the VIP cancer lounge, we overheard a peculiar request from the young woman to her mother. It became a running joke for the remainder of my treatment. Very seriously, she asked if, after chemo, they could go to Restoration Hardware and get lobster rolls. Yes, the upscale furniture store that sells $16,000 chandeliers. In certain show-rooms of theirs, such as the one in Nashville near the fancy chemo infusion center, they also have an upscale restaurant inside of them.

There's so much to break down here.

First, anyone who has gone through chemo or watched a show where someone has gone through chemo knows that the accompanying stomach stuff can be tough. So you're telling me that right after you get pumped full of toxic chemicals, you want to add fish and mayonnaise to the mix? That doesn't sound nauseating at all!

And Restoration Hardware? That is very specific. A restaurant inside of a fancy furniture store. Why there? Why their lobster roll? How did you become aware of this crustacean delicacy? How do you know that in a city of world-class restaurants, *this* is the best one?

Who are you that this is just a casual request for your post-chemo routine?

Can we be friends?

. . .

Without fail, after every chemo session, I would ask David if we could go for lobster rolls. We both knew that I was 100% joking. Even on the day that I got to ring the bell for being done with chemo, sort of, I couldn't even fathom a celebration lunch. The Red Devil was that evil. We WERE going, however at some point. I was just waiting for the opportune moment to make it happen. One day it wouldn't just be a joke. We would go and treat ourselves to a $36 lobster roll. We deserved it.

So skip ahead about six months. I've finished chemo, had my surgery, and am on my final day of radiation. I am finally DONE with active treatment. It was that day that I decided we were going to fulfill my months-long dream to experience the Restoration Hardware lobster roll.

This was a big day. It was the end of over nine months of treatment. Radiation was exhausting, and it was over. It was time to start healing, and if I was lucky, start to return to some sense of normal. There was no way I was not going to ring the bell. I finished my radiation session, and the techs that I had been working with walked me towards the exit where the bell was. A group of nurses was waiting there for me. They read me a cheesy poem, and I rang that bell like there was no tomorrow.

After I rang the bell, this time for real, we got in the car for the 15-minute drive south to the fancy Restoration Hardware. I had, of course, made a reservation and let them know that this was a celebratory lunch marking the end of my nine-month cancer battle. I was deserving of the world's best lobster roll. (Certainly, the world's most expensive.) We were greeted with a glass of champagne and all the fanfare of a celebrity. We ordered the lobster roll.

Final take, Restoration Hardware's lobster roll was almost worth going through cancer for.

Chapter Twenty-eight

Back to the Sushi Restaurant

When I went to the follow-up appointment with my oncologist after radiation, I was having flashbacks about the time I thought I was done with chemo but wasn't. She did her typical physical exam, went over my labs, then she turned to me and said, "Well that's it. I'll see you next June." This was August.

I was stunned. This person who I had seen just about weekly for over six months was sending me on my way. I had one last question, "When am I considered in remission?"

I wasn't expecting it when she said, "Well we don't call it 'remission,' but you are No Evidence of Disease, or N.E.D.."

Floored. Nine months of hell after the most life-up-ending diagnosis. And that was it.

I gave her a hug and said, "I'll miss you. But not really." Then I walked to the checkout desk and I started crying. I wasn't expecting that wave of emotions, but it just hit me. The people around me thought something was wrong. But these were happy tears!

That night we needed to make things come full circle, so we took the kids back to the fancy sushi restaurant to tell them the news.

We didn't tell them we were celebrating. We just walked in and sat down. With straight faces, we looked at them very seriously and said, "We have something we need to tell you . . ."

"Mommy is cancer-free!"

I got the BIGGEST high-five from our now ten-year-old. A kid who usually doesn't show a lot of emotion. The best part is that he totally got the joke and meaning of us taking them back to the sushi restaurant. In character, the five-year-old just asked if she could have my phone.

So much had changed, and yet, so much was exactly the same.

The waiter did overhear the good news, but sadly, this time there were no free dishes brought to our table.

David was disappointed that we didn't get any freebies and I was sad my cancer card had been revoked. Time to go back to normal life.

Chapter Twenty-nine

Barbie Boobs

As luck would have it, I would finish my cancer treatment and be officially N.E.D. (cancer free) with a few months to spare for my fortieth birthday. While there aren't many silver linings to breast cancer, there are a few, and one of them is a federal law that requires that insurance companies pay for reconstruction after mastectomy.

There are a number of options when it comes to reconstruction (including doing none at all). The choices range from aesthetic flat closure, where you decide to indefinitely stay flat; to silicone implants; to DIEP Flap reconstruction. My choice was DIEP Flap surgery, an extremely intricate surgery that takes six to ten hours with two plastic surgeons who remake your breasts from your abdomen. Just to be clear: *essentially, they use the fat, skin, and blood vessels from a tummy tuck to remake your boobs.* Hell yes!

As my plastic surgeon said, "You might as well get something out of this." Nearly a year after I ended active treatment, I would be on the road to having my twenty-eight year old body back. I couldn't ask for a better birthday present.

When surgery day arrived, I was very nervous. Not only is this a major surgery, it also meant being under for a very long time. It's nearly impossible not to think that there's a chance that I might not wake up. Again, how cruel would that be after everything else that I'd gone through. Before rolling me back to the operating room, the usual parade of doctors happened. Each going over what their role in the room would be. Finally my plastic surgeon, Dr. Megan Vucovich (I trusted her instantly since she spells Megan the right way), came in, and she made some marks on my body. Then she asked if I was ready, and I responded with "go big or go home!". Then I told her to feel free to take as much fat from my abdomen as possible. We had a laugh and then it was time.

Nine hours later I started to wake up in the ICU. I would be there for the next 48 hours, so that the heartbeat to my new boob babies could be monitored hourly to ensure that the skin flaps moved from my abdomen to create my new breasts were working. This was done with a small doppler machine that would seek out my heartbeat where the veins and blood vessels had been connected to keep my new boobs alive. It sounded exactly like the heartbeat of a developing baby in utero - a beautiful sound you sit with bated breath waiting to hear each time it's checked.

I was told by the nurse that as I was waking up one of the surgeons was explaining that everything went great, and they also fixed two hernias while they were in there (thank you to Eva who was an eleven pound baby when she was born!). To which, I thanked them profusely. I have no recollection of this, but apparently it was very enduring. A little while later the nurses were checking my breasts and they described them as "Barbie boobs". They informed me that they were some of the best boobs that they had ever seen come out of this procedure. Even more fitting, given that I have no nipples, just like Barbie. (Those will likely come later in the form of tattoos.) Later, one of the more junior surgeons who was checking on me, also informed me that my abdomen looked like a Hollywood cosmetic job.

Let me stress, this is not a reason to get cancer (as if it's a choice). The recovery from this takes four to eight weeks. Coming out of surgery, my breasts looked like they'd won fight club, barely. After being on a respirator for nine hours, I could barely take in a full breath of aire for days. In my first walk down a short hallway and back after the surgery, I thought I was going to die. When I flopped back into the chair in my room, I was wheezing heavily. It is not a walk in the park. In six to twelve months there will be another surgery to even them out and get them as close to "natural" as possible.

All of that said, if you are going to get breast cancer, then why not walk away with Barbie Boobs and a flat tummy? This time, instead of doing what I have to in order to survive, I am doing this for me. Hopefully, this is the last major step in this journey.

Chapter Thirty

Not Dead Yet

The celebrations didn't end at lobster rolls, sushi or new boobs. Having been part of the cancer community for almost a year at this point, there was a little inside joke that I decided to bring my circle into. Every year on your cancer-versary (the annual celebration of still being alive) people adorn themselves with #notdeadyet head-bands, cakes, T-shirts, and tiaras. They throw themselves a little party and invite no one, or everyone. To each, it's personal. But it's important. It's another year of life you are lucky to have. It's a year further from the horrible journey of cancer, or for some, a year they are still alive. For me, as each of those years ticks on, there's a lower chance that the cancer will return.

For my celebration on finishing a marathon of treatments, I decided to treat myself and our close friends to a "Not Dead Yet" cake (actual image is on the front cover of the book) that I had ordered from the Publix bakery. Just a simple round vanilla cake with pink frosting, a few celebratory balloons, and in black icing the words "Not Dead Yet." I ordered the cake online and went to the bakery to pick it up. When the baker handed it to me, she just chuckled. I have no idea if she truly understood the joke and was in on it. Maybe she thought it was some dark humor for a friend turning fifty. It didn't matter.

I took the cake home, lined up the champagne bottles and glasses for those that could celebrate in person, and got my computer ready for the series of Zoom calls I had set up for those that couldn't. Every fifteen or thirty minutes I would get on a new Zoom call with the different groups of people who had been cheering me on through this journey. My close family. My college girlfriends. The Countertop Club. Our Nashville friends popped in and out one-by-one for some cake and a toast.

Not everyone appreciated the dark humor of my cake. My Aunt Colleen being one of them, since she had lost her son, my cousin Brian, just over a year earlier. At the young age of forty-two, with a soon-to-be fiancé, and a whole life ahead of him, he had a massive heart attack and was gone. I understand why there was nothing funny about her niece still being alive after a battle with cancer. I totally get it.

I get that there will be people who will find nothing funny in this book. Despite moments of respite, the shadow of cancer will always overpower. We each manage and process in our own way.

That said, I look forward to my annual "Not Dead Yet" cake and any reason to celebrate with friends and family. Life is fragile. Honestly, you never know when that time will be gone.

Epilogue

As I was writing this book, about six months after I finished treatment, there was this crazy conspiracy with Kate Middleton, the Princess of Wales.

In case you missed it because you were living on an Amish farm, or not old enough to care yet, she went in for a mysterious abdominal surgery in January. This surgery required a ten-day stay in the hospital. To put this into perspective, my double mastectomy was supposed to be a one-night stay, but it turned into two. Whatever happened with her surgery to require ten nights in the hospital was pretty major.

No one saw her leave the hospital. Then Prince William canceled an appearance and speech at his godfather's funeral. Things got weird, and the theories got weirder.

Was she dead? Was she in a coma? Did she get pregnant by another man, while William fathered a different child with a different woman?

Then came the Mother's Day photo that she supposedly released. The internet sleuths immediately identified a series of inconsistencies with the photo. Their daughter Charlotte's hand looked weird. Other things looked off.

The plot thickened. The conspiracies went rogue. My favorite: the royal family had done her off.

Then she finally appeared in a video released by the palace and announced that it was just cancer.

Not a kidnapping. Not a mysterious death or affair. Just plain old boring cancer. Like a typical forty-something woman.

She just wanted some privacy to process what was happening and figure out how to talk to her young children about it while reassuring them that she was going to be okay.

Too bad my book wasn't published yet, or she would have known what to do.

• • •

Anyway, there is no end to this story, I hope, because if there is I'm probably dead.

Once all my active treatment was over and I was recovering, I knew that things were back to normal when my chin hair, Freida, showed back up. She's been a staple of my chin for many years. Reliably coming back every few weeks. Growing long enough for me to pluck her. And then, like clockwork, she makes her way back.

She disappeared during chemo with the rest of my hair. I'm not sure I can say I missed her, but when she returned, I knew that it was time to move on with life.

My hair has been growing back slowly, and I've been going through my various eras. The Cute Baby Hair Era. The Hedgehog Era. The Mullet Era. The Nineties Gymnast Era. The Lesbian Era. It's taking a lot longer than I had imagined. I guess I didn't really think through how long it takes to grow out a full head of locks. But I'll get there. I even finally took the leap, and with permission from Baz, went blonde. So far, I am having more fun, and think I'll stay this way for a while.

Some things in my life have become more important, while others have been deprioritized. Take for instance, my eyebrows. They are much more important than they used to be. What were once some hairs on my face that I would occasionally pluck, now have their own routine and just this week I spent $34 on an eyebrow pencil. Who am I?

I'm a little more carefree than I used to be. I don't let the little things get to me, and I do things that might have been considered out of character before cancer. Like writing a book. This is my third or fourth concept, but I've finally made it happen because, well, cancer.

I'd be remiss also not to mention one more time the outpouring of love and support that we received from our family and friends throughout this whole journey. There were the letters and the gifts. There were visits from friends who made a point to come see us and take care of us during one of the hardest periods of our lives. There was my mom, who despite being scared to death of what was happening, came to be there for us when I started chemo, when I had my mastectomy and again when I had my reconstruction surgery.

Then there was a trip to Paris. Just when I thought that there was no possible way the world could be more generous to me and my family, the most unbelievable thing happened. Family friends sent me and David on an all-expense paid trip to Paris. No kids. Just us reconnecting in the city of love, surrounded by beauty and hopefully closing a chapter for good. No cancer. No worries. Just eight full days of being carefree. For the first time in over a year, no one there knew what we had gone through. I no longer looked like a cancer patient. And we just got to go back to being David and Megan on an adventure together. Truly the gift of a lifetime.

The distance between me and cancer continues to grow. While it always will be a part of who I am and my experience, I hope that it was just a blip in the timeline . . . a thing that pushed me out of my comfort zone into things like writing a book and pursuing my comedy career. I will never be grateful for having cancer, but I will thank cancer for giving the perspective and motivation to make the most of it all.

In the words of a contest judge who left comments on an excerpt from this book, *"This was well written, but I thought the only funny line was at the end. I hope all goes well with your boob journey!"*

Thank you,

I hope all goes well with my boob journey too!

Acknowledgements

You never know how a spouse is going to react when cancer enters the scene. David didn't flinch. Not only was he by my side through nine months of cancer treatment, but he is the reason that this book is here. Thank you for the relentless encouragement and support in making this happen.

While my family was around the country, it never felt like it. My mom made many trips to Nashville throughout treatment to take care of me, and help with the kids. She was also my first line editor, making the book stronger and helping me through the process. Aunt Sue and Uncle Randy, I know you are all too familiar with the tolls of cancer, and cannot thank you enough for your insider guidance and showers of love through the journey.

To my tribe that I didn't fully realize existed before this happened. You fueled my ability to be positive throughout and beyond cancer treatment. There are too many people to name, but I'm going to try: Kim, Sam, Talitha, Ling Ling, Katie, Erin, Amelia, Ann, Brad, Jackie, Pat, Angie, Saba, Colleen, Derek, Megan, Kyle, Alison, Allyson, Barb, Emma, Kelly, Lisa, Olga, Mary, Nathalie, Tracy. Thank you for laughing with me and providing love through it all.

My beta readers, Jef and Kelsey, your words of encouragement and support in writing this book means so much to me. Especially under the circumstances of losing your dear Annika to cancer. You have my indefinite love and gratitude.

Doug, thank you for allowing me to put on paper the ultimate dark humor cancer story. I wish that we had gotten to know Cathy more before tragedy struck. She was clearly an amazing human.

Thank goodness I worked at Indeed when Cancer happened. Jennifer, your support from day one will never be forgotten. For the beta reading turned proofreading, thank you Alisha. To all of my work family colleagues who checked in on me, supported me, and picked up my slack through those nine months, particularly, Jessica, Tyler, Sumita, Shruti, Jennifer O., Greta, Janeane, Anwar, Money Megan, Cliona, Eoin, Brittany, Carmen, Landrea, Ruth, Thad, James, & Russell. Y'all are the best!

For the book publishing guidance and final edit, thank you Brian Kannard. Your guidance strengthened this book into what it is, and it wouldn't be truly real without your help. Thank you.

Made in the USA
Columbia, SC
09 September 2024

41451263R00093